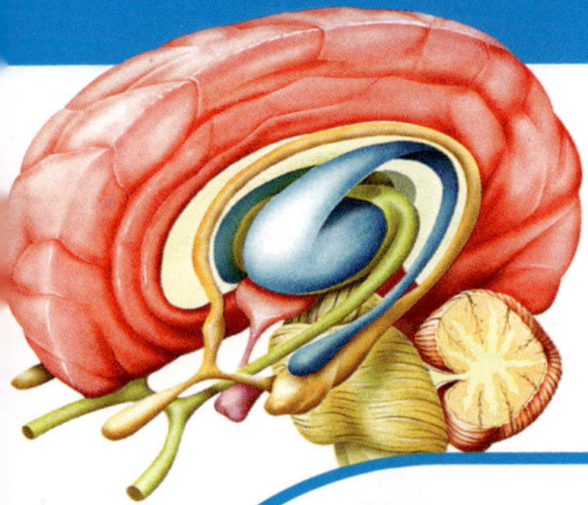

TELL ME ABOUT ?

GOLDEN MINDS

GOLDEN MINDS PUBLISHING HOUSE

TELL ME ABOUT

ISBN 978-81-8341-477-7

Published by:
Golden Minds Publishing House
326-330, Vardhaman Chambers,
Cawasji Patel Road, Kala Ghoda,
Fort, Mumbai - 400 001
Tel: 022 22821704 / 1705
email: goldenminds99@gmail.com

Printed in India.

CONTENTS

PREHISTORIC WORLD

AMAZING EARTH

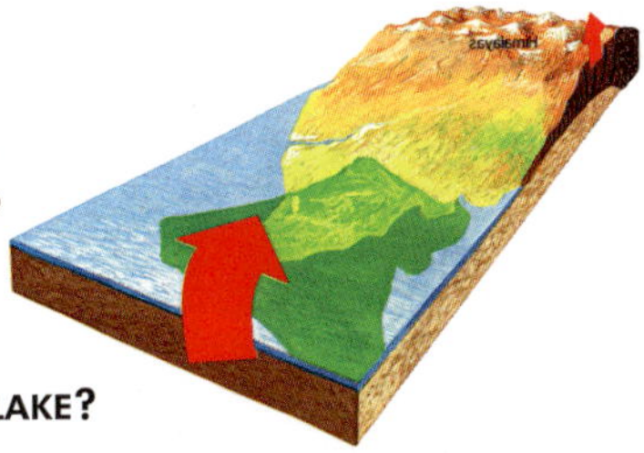

SCIENCE AND TECHNOLOGY

CONTENTS

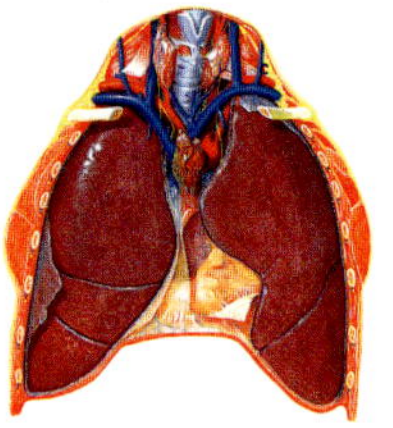

What Do you know about the Nest and Eggs of a Dinosaur?

The eggs of most of the dinosaurs were elongated. They had flexible shells like stiff leather. They were small in size and looked very much like the eggs of a bird. Some were about the size of a large potatoe. The nests of many Protoceratops were found in a small area which indicates that these dinosaurs bred in colonies. The nests were shallow bowl-shaped pits about 1m across. They were scraped in dry, sandy earth and surrounded by low walls. The female Protoceratops laid a clutch of 20 or so tough-shelled sausage-shaped eggs. The eggs were arranged in a circular or spiral shape like the spokes of a wheel. The nest and eggs of the Orodromeus, a small plant-eater, have been found in Montana, USA. Its eggs were also arranged in a spiral form.

BITS OF FACT

The largest dinosaur's egg discovered is that of the Hypselosaurus. Its egg measured about 1 foot long and 10 inches wide.

What do you know about The Neolithic Period?

The Neolithic Period is marked by such innovations as the cultivation of plants and rise of urban civilization. With the beginning of agricultural production by man, there was a problem that man had to deal with. He did not know how to protect his crops from animals and enemies. So, he had to leave the caves and rock shelters that he previously lived in. He built homes to stay within a close distance from his farm so that he could keep his eyes on his farm. However, Neolithic houses were built adjacent to one another. This arrangement of houses was a sort of defence system. Neolithic people built single-storey houses in rectangular shapes, supported by wooden beams and buttresses. Most houses were built with flat roofs that provided working space where they prepared their food. Interestingly, houses did not have doors but were entered through openings in the roofs that they reached using wooden ladders. They also decorated their walls with spectacular paintings which depicted religious figurines, death and incarnation, hunting, wild animals, flowers, geometric patterns, imprints of hands, stars etc.

BITS OF FACT

The settlements at Cayonu, Catalhoyuk, Hacilar, Norsuntepe and Kosk represent typical Neolithic towns. Although Catalhoyuk in Central Turkey is the most advanced among all, but Cayonu in the Eastern Turkey dates back to around 7,250-6,750 BCE which makes it the oldest Neolithic village in Turkey.

What do you know about the Bronze Age?

The Bronze Age is the time period that marks a significant development in the human culture, before the introduction of iron, when most tools and weapons were made of bronze. In order to make their lives easier, humans were inventing new things. They learnt to alloy copper with tin that makes a harder and stronger metal than both copper and tin. We call this metal bronze and this period of time is called the Bronze Age. This period falls almost within the same period of time when the writing was invented in Mesopotamia. The invention of bronze led to the development of new skills in processing and refining gold, silver and other metals. The artifacts made out of a mixture of gold and silver have decorated the palaces of Kings and Princes over the years. The significant increase in the production and surplus of metal products has necessitated the export of such items to other communities in the area or even to other kingdoms in remote areas. Another important invention of this period was that of carts of four wheels drawn by oxen which had provided significant assistance during transport.

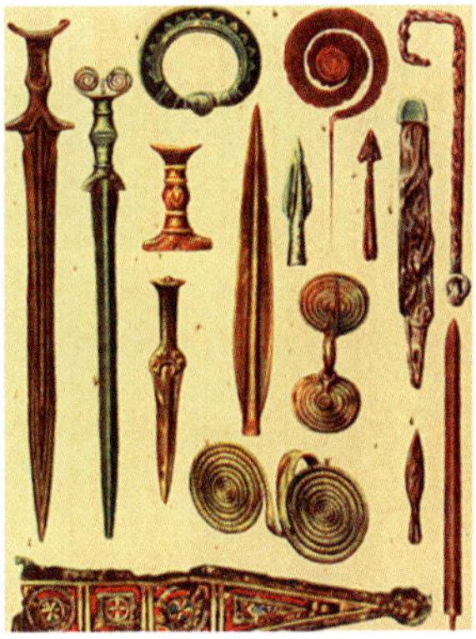

BITS OF FACT

For the first time, the Indian bronze statue appeared in the form of a dancing girl in the Harappan Age. The statue is noted for its excellent craftsmanship.

What do you know about the skin of a dinosaur?

Several fossils of the skins of dinosaurs have been found which reveal that they had scales similar to the ones that the reptiles of today have. Also, no one knows about the colour of the dinosaur's skin. Some experts believe that dinosaurs were similar in colour to crocodiles – dull green and brown. The first fossil of the dinosaur's skin was found in the mid-1800s. Initially, experts thought that the skin was of the giant prehistoric crocodile. The scales of the dinosaur were embedded in its thick, tough, leathery skin as in the crocodile. Scaly skin protected the dinosaur from the teeth and claws of enemies and bites of small pests, such as mosquitoes and fleas. The scales on the skins of dinosaurs were roughly six-sided, like the cells in a bee's honeycomb. The fossil skin of the Edmontosaurus, a duckbill Hadrosaur, was found. It reveals that the dinosaur was covered in thousands of small pebble-like scales with large lumps or tubercles spaced among them.

BITS OF FACT

The skins of both the Hadrosaurus and the Edmontosaurus had a leathery pebbled appearance, somewhat like that of a football. Other ornithopods display a skin texture similar to that of the modern gila monster.

What do you know about the young ones of dinosaurs?

In 1978, the fossils of the Maiasaura were found in Montana, USA. Maiasaura was a duckbill dinosaur or Hadrosaur. Fifteen babies along with many broken eggshells were found scattered around a large mound-shaped structure. The nest was about 2m across and covered with vegetation. The teeth of the babies found in the nest were slightly worn away. This indicated that they were not new born. They had eaten food. Evidence from these nesting sites indicates that dinosaurs were caring parents. They protected and fed their young ones. In the Gobi desert, the Protoceratop, a pig-sized dinosaur, dug holes in the sand and buried the eggs. The female left them to hatch in the heat of the sand, while she herself protected them from predators.

BITS OF FACT

The most spectacular fact about the Microraptor is that it had not one, but two sets of primitive wings - one on its forearms and one on its hind legs.

WHAT DO YOU KNOW ABOUT THE SIZE OF THE BRAIN OF A DINOSAUR?

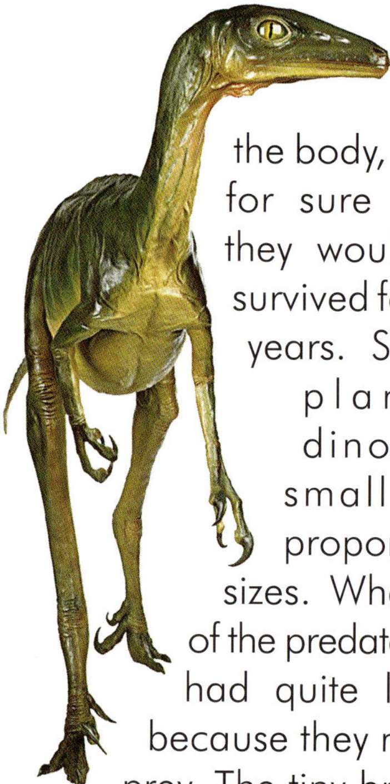

There is a broad link between the size of an animal's brain, when compared to the size of the body, and the level of intelligence it shows. We know for sure that dinosaurs were intelligent, otherwise they would not have survived for millions of years. Some of the plant-eating dinosaurs had small brains in proportion to their sizes. Whereas, some of the predatory dinosaurs had quite large brains because they needed to think quickly as they went after their prey. The tiny brain of the Stegosaurus weighed about 70-80 gm, whereas the whole dinosaur weighed up to 2 tons. The cleverest dinosaur was the Troodon, which was just the size of a large domestic dog. Its brain was very large in proportion to its size. Its brain was about 1/100th the weight of its whole body. It could run very fast, swerve and duck to catch its prey.

BITS OF FACT

The brain of the Stegosaurus was only 1/25,000th the weight of its whole body. In a human, it is 1/50th. The brain of the Brachiosaurus was only 1/100,000th the weight of its whole body.

WHAT DO YOU KNOW ABOUT THE TEETH ARRANGEMENT OF THE MEGALODON?

The Megalodon appeared in pre-historic oceans during the Oligocene Period. It ruled the oceans for 20 million years. It was similar to the present-day sharks, but much larger in size, about 65 feet, as tall as a six-storey building. The term Megalodon originated from the Greek word 'mega' meaning big and 'odon' meaning tooth. Hence, the megalodon means a dinosaur with a big tooth. It had hundreds of finely serrated and razor-sharp teeth which were spread over in 3 to 5 rows. The first two rows were used to grasp the prey. It could swallow huge chunks at a time. If the teeth were broken, lost or worn out, the other rows would take their place. Its jaws were about 3 metres wide. Scientists have estimated this huge size from the sizes of the fossilised teeth and the fossilised jaws that have been found.

BITS OF FACT

You could drive a car through a set of Megalodon's dentures without scraping off the paint. The Megalodon became extinct about 2 million years ago due to the cooling of the oceans. The fossils of the Megalodon's teeth and jaws were found only in the regions that had predominantly warm water environments.

What do you know about the speeds of dinosaurs?

The speed of a dinosaur can be estimated using the distance between the footprints and the leg length. The huge Apatosaurus and the other Sauropods had short legs and were probably among the slowest of the dinosaurs. Massive, heavily plated dinosaurs, like the Ankylosaurids,

were also among the slowest of the dinosaurs. The bird-like, bipedal carnivores (Theropods) which had long, slim hind-limbs, and light bodies are believed to be the speediest dinosaurs. These dinosaurs used their short, feathered arms to help speed up their running by gliding from trees to the ground. However, these fast dinosaurs weren't much faster than modern-day land animals. The following speeds were calculated by R. A. Thulborn (1982, University of Queensland, Australia): The Sauropodamorphs had a speed of 5 km/h, the Stegosaurs and the Ankylosaurs had speeds of 6-8 km/h. Most Sauropods walked about 12-17 km/h, with a maximum speed of 20-30 km/h. Large Theropods and Ornithopods achieved 20 km/h, the Ceratopsians achieved 25 km/h, small Theropods and Ornithopods reached 40km/h and the Ornithomimids reached 60 km/h.

BITS OF FACT

The Ornithomimus was a fast, agile dinosaur, which could run about as quickly as an ostrich. It ran approximately up to 43 miles per hour

What do know about the extinction of dinosaurs?

The dinosaurs came to a fairly sudden end 65 million years ago. Many other reptiles such as pterosaurs and plesiosaurs also disappeared. Several theories are put forth regarding the extinction of dinosaurs. One theory suggests that the continents were drifting apart continuously during the late Cretaceous Period. It resulted in a huge increase in volcanic activities. The hot lava and gases from these volcanoes filled the air with poisonous fumes to such high levels that they affected the dinosaurs and their sources of food *i.e.* plant. Another theory says that a giant meteorite from space hit the Earth which caused volcanoes. These volcanoes threw up vast amounts of dust and darkened the skies. Skies darkened by dust lasted for more than a year which meant the death of plants and, hence, the death of plant-eating animals. This eventually led to the death of flesh-eating dinosaurs who depended on the plant-eaters.

BITS OF FACT

Scientists have found a huge crater - the Chixulub Crater- under the seabed off the coast of Yucatan, Mexico. This could be the place where the giant meteorite hit the Earth 65 million years ago

What do you know about the Homo sapiens or wise man?

Scientists have discovered that the Homo sapiens had a skeleton shaped like the human skeleton of today. His brain was actually larger than the human brain of today. This early man was both a hunter and gatherer. He created stone tools, bone needles and bone fish hooks. He sewed clothes from animal skins with thread made from the other parts of the animal. He also made warm boots. One of the species of the Homo sapiens was the Homo Neandertals. They were much taller, very strong and marvellous hunters. They buried the dead with ceremony which suggests they might have had religious beliefs. The discoveries of Neandertal grave sites show that they decorated their bodies with paint, possibly for religious reasons or perhaps for beauty. These sites provide the first evidence of the use of colours by them. The evidence also suggests that the Neandertals were the first to think about the possibility of an afterlife.

BITS OF FACT

The Neanderthal man was named after the valley, Neander, in which the skeleton of an old man was discovered. The Neanderthals died out around 30,000 B.C.

What do you know about the cave paintings of the Cro-Magnon man?

The Cro-Magnon man painted marvellous and astonishing paintings on rock walls within their caves. Each cave had hundreds of different paintings by many different painters. Most of these cave paintings focussed on hunters and various animals. Natural colours were used by the early man. He even used charcoal to create these paintings besides using mineral pigments like iron oxide (red ochre) and black manganese. Besides the figures of people and animals, the other objects found in cave paintings were the stencils of hands. It is believed that the Cro-Magnon man, after creating his paintings on the cave walls, put his hand against the cave wall and outlined it with charcoal or paint. When you think of a cave, you may figure it out as a big place with high ceilings. Actually, it was not so during that time. The Cro-Magnon man crawled on his belly through the mazes of narrow, dark tunnels to the places where cave paintings have been found. The marvellous paintings were hidden deep within the darkest portions of the cave.

BITS OF FACT

Like many discoveries, the cave paintings were discovered accidentally. The caves in Lascaux, France, were found around 1940 during World War II by a few kids. They stumbled across the entrance to a cave that had been hidden by the roots of a tree.

WHAT DO YOU KNOW ABOUT THE SIZES OF DINOSAURS?

Dinosaurs varied in sizes greatly. Some were only about the size of a chicken or even smaller. One of the smallest dinosaur was the Compsognathus, which was slim, with a long, narrow tail. It was just 70 cm in length and weighed less than 3 kg. This dinosaur lived during the late Jurassic Period about 155-150 million years ago and had small, sharp curved teeth. It moved through the under-growth. It fed on insects, spiders and worms. The biggest dinosaurs were the Sauropods such as the Brachiosaurus and the Argentinosaurus. The Brachiosaurus was a plant-eater with a length of 25 m from nose to tail. Its weight is estimated to vary from 30 to 75 tonnes. It had huge front legs and a long neck which could reach food more than 13 m from the ground. It had small chisel-shaped teeth for snipping leaves from trees. The Argentinosaurus from South America weighed about 100 tons or more.

BITS OF FACT

The biggest carnivorous (meat-eating) dinosaurs were the Theropods. The Giganotosaurus Carolinii was 47 feet long, 8 tons in weight and 12 feet tall. It had enormous jaws with 8-inch long serrated teeth in a 6-foot (1.8 m) long skull.

WHAT DO YOU KNOW ABOUT THE MESOLITHIC AGE?

The name "Mesolithic" comes from two separate words. The word Mesos means Middle and 'Lithos' means Stone. When climatic conditions began to change in the Mesolithic period, animals and humans were forced to adapt themselves to new environmental conditions. Animals became smaller in sizes and faster than before. So, humans had to develop their stone tools and weapons in a more practical form. Hunting and the collection of plants continued to be the main supply of food, but the humans began to store their food in storages for later consumption. More tools and weapons were made of bones and wood. One of the most interesting usages of stone of this period is what is called Microliths that were small tools made of Obsidian and flints. The domestication of animals was the main development of this period; the dog was domesticated during the Mesolithic Age. From the wall paintings, we understand that the artistic qualifications of this period are almost equal to preceding Old Stone Age.

BITS OF FACT

Another characteristic of the Mesolithic period were hunting and fishing, settlements along rivers and on lake shores where fish and molluscs were abundant.

What do you know about the dinosaurs that protected themselves?

Dinosaurs had various ways of protecting themselves. Some dinosaurs were too big to be brought down and eaten. Some could run very fast, like the ostrich dinosaurs which could attain speeds of 70 km/hr. and could escape their predators. The slow-moving dinosaurs were usually covered with spikes or horns to protect themselves. Many kinds of dinosaurs had protective armours which took the form of bony plates embedded in their skins. The Saltasaurus had hundreds of small bony lumps, each as big as a pea, packed together in the skin of its back. The Stegosaurus had several large roughly triangular shaped bony plates along its back. These stood upright in two rows. They were probably used to control the body temperature. The tail had four large spikes which were used for self-defence. The Sauropelta had a row of sharp spikes along each side of its body from head to tail to protect it from its enemies.

BITS OF FACT

Many meat-eating dinosaurs had long and sharp claws on their fingers. The Deinocheirus had the longest claws. Its massive finger claws were more than 35 cm long.

What do You know about the Egyptian Civilization?

The Egyptian civilization flourished on the banks of River Nile about 3,000 years before Christ. No other civilization has captured the imagination of scholars and archaeologists so much. The Egyptians believed that the body and soul were important for human existence in life and in death. The graves were filled with food, tools, domestic ware, treasures - all the necessities of life so that the deceased might live happily in another world. Stone and clay pots comprise one of the most important categories of Egyptian artifacts. The banks of River Nile provided the mud and clay used to make ceramic ware in those times. Food was cooked in clay pots, which also served as containers for grains, water, wine,

beer, flour and oils. Baskets were also found in their homes. They were made from reeds and the leaves of date palms that grew along the Nile.

BITS OF FACT

The Egyptian language was one of the earliest languages to be written down. Only the Sumerian language is older.

WHAT DO YOU KNOW ABOUT THE VIKINGS' TRAVELS?

The Vikings hailed from Scandinavia and Denmark, and ruled the northern seas from the 8th to the 11th centuries. Their travels carried

them extensively. It has been proven that they did, in fact, reach North America almost 500 years before Columbus' alleged "discovery" of the West Indies. They were fierce sea-raiders who fared much better at sea-battles than on land. Although they were more interested in establishing trade routes rather than looting and pillaging cities, yet they did raid several sea ports. They had an intricate and surprisingly sophisticated civilization during their time. They discovered North America nearly 500 years before Columbus. They called the land of their discovery "Vinland" which is now believed to be present-day Newfoundland in Canada. They were heathens (non-Christians) in a period of time in which the rest of Europe was largely Christianized.

BITS OF FACT

The Vikings were able to navigate with the use of a mineral called the "sun stone", which, found native to their shores, had the ability to polarize sunlight. It made possible for them to use the sun in order to navigate even during the heaviest cloud-cover.

What do you know about the Mayan civilization?

The Mayan civilization reached its peak from about AD 300 to AD 900, which is known as the Classic period. It thrived for more than 2,000 years. The people known as the Maya lived in the region that is now eastern and southern Mexico, Guatemala, Belize, El Salvador and western Honduras. The Maya built massive stone pyramids, temples and sculpture, developed a system of writing using hieroglyphs and recorded their achievements in mathematics and astronomy. The earliest Maya were farmers who lived in small, scattered villages of pole and thatch houses. Slowly, society became more complex with the development of distinct social classes. At the top of society, a hereditary king ruled over each Maya city. The most distinctive Mayan achievement was in mathematics and astronomy. They introduced a pair of interlocking calendars, which were used to schedule ceremonies. One calendar was based on the sun and contained 365 days.

BITS OF FACT

Chichén Itzá was a very large city with a central area covering about 5 sq km (2 sq miles). Its architecture shows the introduction of columns, wider rooms and doorways, and sloping zones around the base of the buildings.

WHAT DO YOU KNOW ABOUT THE AZTEC CIVILIZATION?

Among the civilizations in Mesoamerica, the Aztec civilization was

among the most advanced civilization. The Aztecs built great cities and developed a complex social, political and religious structure. Their capital, Tenochtitlán, was located on the site of present-day Mexico City. Tenochtitlán was the centre of the Aztec world. The marvels of the island city were described at length by the Spanish conquerors who called it the "Venice of the New World" because of its many canals. Aztec society was highly structured, based on agriculture, and guided by a religion that pervaded every aspect of life. The Aztecs worshipped gods

that represented natural forces which they believed were vital to their agricultural economy. Aztec cities were dominated by giant stone pyramids topped by temples where human sacrifices were dedicated to the gods. In the Aztec empire, some manufactured goods were produced for the ruler or sold in the local markets. These included pottery, tools, jewellery, figurines, baskets and cloth.

BITS OF FACT

One of the most famous surviving Aztec sculptures is the so-called calendar stone, which weighs 22 metric tons and measures 3.7 m (12 ft) in diameter. The calendar stone represents the Aztec universe. The face of the Aztec Sun-god is carved in the centre.

WHAT DO YOU KNOW ABOUT THE TIME ZONES AROUND THE WORLD?

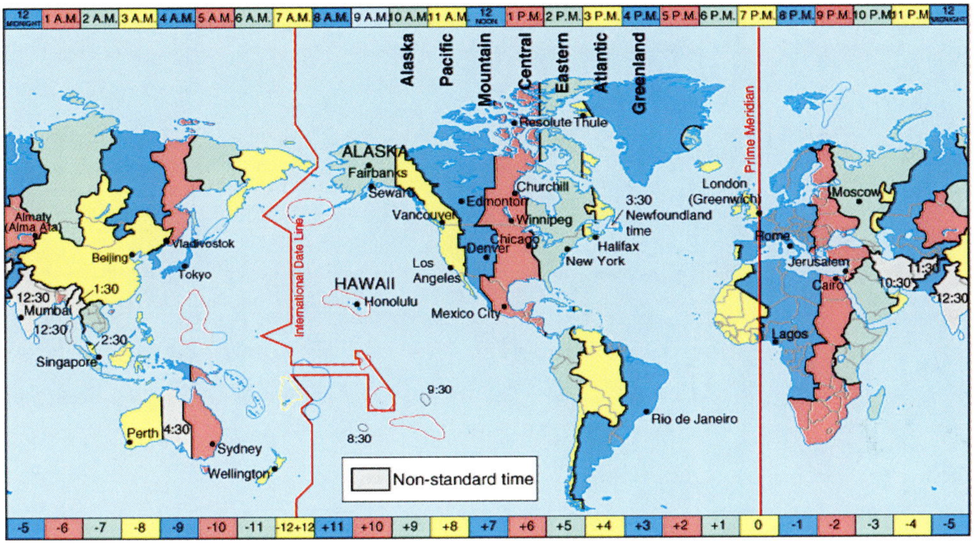

The Earth rotates 15 degrees longitude per hour. Hence, the Earth's 360 degrees are divided into 24 zones. Each measures about 15 degrees in width. The 0 degree longitude line or meridian is defined as a line running through the Old Greenwich Observatory in Greenwich, England. Time in each of the 12 zones east of Greenwich increases by one hour for each zone. Time in each of the 12 zones west of Greenwich decreases by one hour. This is how the time differs around the world. The daily rotation of the Earth is somewhat irregular and is slowing down slightly. Atomic clocks constitute a much more stable time-base. On 1st January, 1972, Greenwich Mean Time (GMT) was replaced as the international time, reference by Co-ordinated Universal Time, maintained by an ensemble of atomic clocks around the world.

BITS OF FACT

Hourly time signals from Greenwich Observatory were first broadcast on 5th February 1924. Greenwich Mean Time (GMT) was established in 1675 when the Royal Observatory was built as an aid to determine longitude at sea by mariners.

What do you know about gemstones?

Gemstones are also known as precious stones. They are minerals that are prized not only for being rare and beautiful but also for their hardness and toughness. Most of the gems are crystals that are formed when magma cools slowly in the Earth's crust. They are found by mining and quarrying or by sifting the mud from the bed of rivers and streams. Gemstones include diamonds, emeralds, rubies and sapphires. The beauty of gems depends to a large extent on their optical properties. A gem cannot be identified by merely looking at it. It is, therefore, necessary to measure its optical properties. The gemologist uses a refractometer to measure the refractive index, which is the relative ability of a gemstone to refract light. In addition to this, another instrument called polariscope is employed to determine whether a gem is doubly or singly refracting. Emeralds, rubies and sapphires are doubly refracting, whereas diamonds are singly refracting.

BITS OF FACT

The biggest natural diamond was dug from a mine in Pretoria, South Africa, on 26th January 1905. It was the Cullinan diamond and weighed 3,106 carats or 621 gm. It was cut into 9 large stones and 96 smaller ones.

WHAT DO YOU KNOW ABOUT DIAMOND?

Diamond is the most prized gems of all. It forms when carbon crystallizes under tremendous heat and pressure, about 100 km below the Earth's surface. The world's largest diamond mine is located in eastern Siberia. It is 525 m deep and 1200 metres in diameter. Diamond is the hardest of all materials and is used not only in jewellery, but also has industrial uses such as drilling and polishing. When a diamond is first mined, it is called a rough diamond. Diamonds vary in shape. Sometimes they have to be split before they are cut and polished. A method called brilliant cutting is employed in cutting most diamonds. This method was invented in the 17th century by an Italian jeweller. The diamond is cut by a revolving metal plate, covered in diamond dust. The faces are angled to reflect as much light as possible.

BITS OF FACT

When Queen Victoria was presented with the Kohinoor diamond, she was disappointed with its sparkle. Then, she had it brilliantly cut. It reduced its weight by nearly 80 carats.

What do you know about tsunami waves?

Tsunamis are gigantic waves that begin when the sea floor is violently shaken by an earthquake, a landslide or a volcanic eruption. Tsunamis travel almost unnoticeably in deep water. As they reach shallow coastal areas, the water piles up into massive waves which can be as high as 30 m and 200 km long. Tsunamis are formed as the displaced water mass moves under the influence of gravity and radiates across the ocean like ripples on a pond. The word 'tsunami' means 'harbour wave' in Japanese because of the way the waves crash into the harbour. Tsunamis usually come in a series with a gap of five minutes or even an hour. When a tsunami hits land, it smashes down onto the shore and washes away houses and people. A tsunami can travel across the sea at a very high speed. Some of these race along at the speed of 900 km/hr, which is as fast as a jet plane. There is often no advance warning of an approaching tsunami. However, an earthquake felt near a body of water may be considered as an indication that a tsunami may shortly follow.

BITS OF FACT

The tsunami at Lituya Bay was the biggest wave ever, but that's just the one humans have witnessed and have been able to record. The waves reached a height of 524 m.

What Do you know about the gold in Seas and oceans?

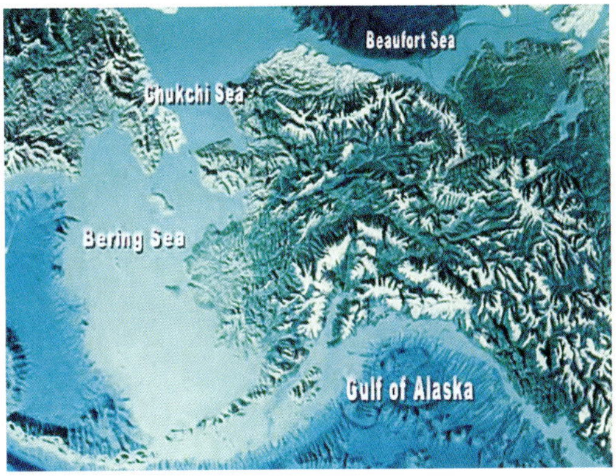

The sea is laden with gold. Where does gold come from? It is leeched out of the place where tectonic plates spread, cold water seeps down into the earth and comes into contact with hot rocks. Unfortunately, it is so dilute that its concentrations or orders of magnitude are smaller than the parts per million. It's more like parts per trillion (ppt). The oceans contain an average gold concentration of about 13 billionths of a gram per litre of seawater (13 ppt). Actually, gold concentration varies between 5 to 50 ppt, depending on location. The Bering Sea contains the highest reported concentration. There are huge deposits of undissolved gold – solid stuff along the mid-ocean ridges of the Atlantic and Pacific Oceans. But the sad part is that it costs too much to mine or extract gold from the sea to make a profit. The concentration of gold in seawater is small. But the cost of pumping the water is greater than the value of the gold. Fort Knox gold mine in Alaska has produced nearly 3.5 million ounces of gold since it went into operation in late 1996.

BITS OF FACT

The ocean contains a small concentration of gold. Such microscopic traces of gold still add up to a lot, which is about 25 billion ounces of gold, worth about 10 trillion dollars. Till now, humans have unearthed only 3 billion ounces of gold.

What do you know about the process of producing silk?

Silk is obtained from silkworms. The species bombyx mori is usually cultivated and raised under controlled environmental and nutritional conditions. The life cycle of a silkworm is as follows: egg, the silkworm, the pupa and the moth. The silkworm which feeds on mulberry leaves forms a covering around it by secreting a protein-like substance through its head.

This stage is called cocoon, a desirable stage for silk producers. The cocoons are sent to a factory where they are first sorted according to their colours, sizes, shapes and textures. Then, they are put through a series of hot and cold immersions so that the sericin or silk gum may be softened. Then, the process of unwinding the silk filaments from the cocoons and combining them together to make a thread of raw silk is done. Finally, the silk filaments are reeled into skeins, which are packed in small bundles called books. Each bundle weighs 2 to 4.5 kg.

BITS OF FACT

When a silkworm makes its cocoon, it spins more than 800 yards of silk in one unbroken length. It can produce 457 to 1,097 metres of thread in just 72 hours.

WHAT DO YOU KNOW ABOUT THE DIFFERENT VARIETIES OF COAL?

Coal is defined as a black or brownish-black solid combustible substance, formed by the partial decomposition of vegetable matter without free access of air and under the continuous influence of moisture and often increased pressure and temperature. It is composed primarily of carbon along with other elements, including sulphur. It is the largest single source of fuel for the generation of electricity world-wide.

There are four types of coal:-

1. Anthracite - This kind of coal has the highest carbon-content. It is a harder, glossy, black coal used primarily for residential and commercial space heating.

2. Bituminous - Bituminous coal has a carboncontent ranging from 45 to 86 per cent. It is a dense coal, usually black, sometimes dark brown, used primarily as fuel in steam-electric power generation.

3. Sub-bituminous - Ranking below bituminous is sub-bituminous coal with 35-45 per cent carbon-content. It is used primarily as fuel for steam-electric power generation.

4. Lignite - Lignite is a geologically young coal which has the lowest carbon-content, *i.e.* 25-35 per cent. It is also referred to as brown coal.

BITS OF FACT

With the world's third largest deposits, China leads the world both in the production and the consumption of coal. The United States has the world's largest known coal reserves.

What do you know about Big Ben?

If you think that the clock in the tower of the Houses of Parliament in Westminster, London, United Kingdom, is called Big Ben, you are wrong. The tower itself is called St. Stephen's Tower, while the clock is called the Westminster clock. It is the bell that strikes the hour which is called the Big Ben. This bell weighs thirteen tons. The tower was built as a part of Charles Barry's design for the new palace, after the old Palace of Westminster was destroyed. The tower is 96.3 metres high. The tower is founded on a 15 by 15 metre raft, made of 3-metre thick concrete, at a depth of 7 metres below the ground level. The four clock faces are 55 metres above the ground. The interior volume of Big Ben is 4,650 cubic metres. The four dials of the clock are 23 square feet, the minute hand is 14 feet long and the figures are 2 feet high. The first 61 metres (250 feet) of the structure is the clock tower, consisting of brickwork with stone cladding. The remainder of the height of the tower is a framed spire of cast iron.

BITS OF FACT

The word 'clock' was first used in the 14th century (about 700 years ago). It comes from the word for bell in Latin ("clocca").

What Do you know about the pearls produced by oysters?

An oyster is a mollusc. It has a soft and very sensitive body inside its hinged shell. Its shell is made of two parts or valves. As the oyster grows in size, its shell also grows. The mantle is an organ that produces the

oyster's shell by using minerals from the oyster's food. The material created by the mantle is called nacre. Nacre lines the inside of the shell. The formation of a pearl begins when a grain of sand or any other substance gets into the soft part of the oyster. In order to protect itself, the oyster covers the irritant with the layers of the nacre – the same substance which makes the shell. The oyster continues to add more and more nacre. Finally, it results in the formation of a pearl. The main component of nacre is the thin layers of the mineral arogonite which is translucent. Light interacts with these overlapping layers to give the finished pearl its lustrous appearance.

BITS OF FACT

The pink or conch pearl is produced by the biggest sea snail, the Strombus Gigas. It is found in the Caribbean and on the Bahamas. It is one of the rarest pearls in the world and its creation is due to a pure chance of Nature.

WHAT DO YOU KNOW ABOUT THE DRIEST PLACE ON THE EARTH?

The driest place on the Earth is the Atacama Desert in South America. This desert covers an area of 966 km, between the Andes Mountain and the Pacific Ocean. Rarely, you can find any vegetation here as the land is blocked from moisture on both sides – one side by the snow-capped Andes Mountains and the other side by the Pacific coastal ranges. As a result, there are salt basins where sand and lava flows. In some parts of the Atacama Desert, no rain has been ever recorded. Very little precipitation (1cm/0.3in per year) that does fall comes from fog. The Atacama Desert covers a total area of 181,300 square km, mostly in Chile, but parts in Peru, Argentina and Bolivia. Still, more than a million people live in the Atacama and crowd around the coastal cities, mining compounds and fishing villages.

BITS OF FACT

The Atacama desert has the rich deposits of copper and other minerals. It also has the world's largset natural supply of sodium nitrate, which was mined until the early 1940s. After the invention of synthetic nitrate in the 20th century, there are about 170 abandoned nitrate mining towns in the desert.

WHAT DO YOU KNOW ABOUT THE WORLD'S HIGHEST NAVIGABLE LAKE?

The world's highest navigable lake is Lake Titicaca. The first steamer to move on the lake was prefabricated in England and carried in pieces on muleback up to the lake in 1862. The lake is about 12,500 feet above the sea level in the Andes Mountains of South America. The lake is the remnant of a vast area of water formed in the Ice Age known as Lake Bolivian. Lake Titicaca is fed by rainwater, *i.e.* the water which melts from the glaciers. The lake covers about 8,300 square km and extends in a northwest-to-southeast direction for a distance of 190 km. At its widest, it is 80 km across. The average depth of the lake is over 100 m with its deepest point at 281 m. About 25 rivers empty their waters into Lake Titicaca. River Ramis, which drains about two-fifths of the entire Titicaca Basin, is the largest. Titicaca's waters are transparent and only slightly brackish, with salinity ranging from 5.2 to 5.5 parts per 1,000. Surface temperatures average 56^{0}F (14 degrees C).

BITS OF FACT

About forty-one islands, some of them densely populated, rise from Titicaca's waters. The largest isTiticaca Island (Spanish: Isla de Titicaca, also called Isla del Sol) which lies just off the tip of the Copacabana Peninsula in Bolivia.

WHAT DO YOU KNOW ABOUT RIVER AMAZON?

In 1539, a large Spanish force started from the town of Quito, in Ecuador, to find out what they could discover towards the east. As their supplies were running out, Gonzalo Pizarro, a brother of the conqueror of Peru, ordered a small group of people to retrace their route by boat and return with fresh supplies. Headed by Francisco de Orellana, the fifty men set off. A strong current hit their boat and forced them eastwards in the opposite direction. They reached a place where trees fringed the edge of the water. There, they were attacked by more than 2,000 natives. After some time, they met a fleet of canoes filled with tall, fair-haired women who shot arrows at them and killed seven of their members. Due to this incident, Orellana named the river 'Amazon' after the race of legendary women warriors. Finally, after a voyage of nearly 4,000 miles, they came to the Atlantic Ocean and became the first men to cross South America at its widest part.

BITS OF FACT

River Nile in Egypt is the longest river. It is 4,145 miles (6,671 km) long and flows into the Mediterranean Sea.

What do you know about the equipment used to measure the depth of an ocean?

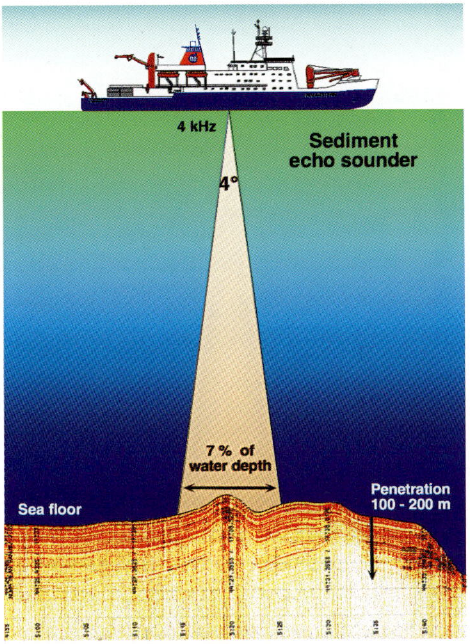

In the olden days, the depth of the ocean was measured by the means of a lead line. A long piece of rope with six foot markings (having a lead weight at the end) was dropped into the water. Then, the depth was measured by noting how much line went down when the lead weight reached the bottom. Later, the depth of an ocean would be determined by sound waves. Modern day oceanographers use sonar instruments to determine the depth of the ocean. A combined transmitter and receiver, called a transducer, sends a sound pulse straight down into the water. The pulse moves down through the water and bounces off the ocean bottom. The transducer is able to pick up the reflected sound. With the help of computers, the time taken for the sound pulse to reach the bottom and return is measured. The depth of the ocean is calculated by knowing how fast sound travels in the water. The sound travels in the water at approximately 1,500 metres per second. This method of seafloor mapping is called echo-sounding.

BITS OF FACT

The largest waterfall on the Earth is actually underwater. It is found in the Denmark Strait and slowly cascades downwards for 2.2 miles. It is over three times as tall as the Angel Falls, in Venezuela, which are the tallest waterfalls.

WHAT DO YOU KNOW ABOUT THE FORMATION OF THE WORLD'S LARGEST DELTA?

A delta is a fertile piece of land near the mouth of some rivers. It is made of the sediments, dumped there by rivers. The world's largest delta is formed by two Himalayan rivers, the Ganges and the Brahmaputra. These two rivers drain into the Bay of Bengal as a combined river carrying the largest amount of sediments. Along with River Meghna, these two rivers have formed one of the largest delta in the world. It is called the Ganges-Brahmaputra Delta or the Bengal Delta. This low-lying fertile plain lies partly in Bangladesh and partly in India. It is also known as the Sunderbans and stretches in a total area of 10,000 square km. Two-thirds of the Sundarbans, *i.e.* 6,000 square kilometres lies in the southwestern delta regions of Bangladesh, whereas the remaining one-third is in India. This delta contains the world's largest area of mangrove forests. It is one of the world's most densely populated areas. Sunderbans is home to the largest number of wild tigers in the world and the biggest colony of the Royal Bengal Tigers.

BITS OF FACT

The second largest mangrove forest is located in Malaysia, but it is just one-tenth the size of mangrove found in the Sunderbans.

WHAT DO YOU KNOW ABOUT THE VARIOUS TYPES OF VOLCANOES?

A volcano is an opening in a planet's surface or crust which allows hot, molten rock, ash and gases to escape from below the surface. The different types of volcanoes are:-

1. Composite volcanoes, also called strato volcanoes, are formed by the alternating layers of lava and rock fragments. Strato volcanoes are usually large and conical.
2. Shield volcanoes may be produced by hot spots which lay far away from the edges of tectonic plates. The eruptions of shield volcanoes are characterized by low explosivity and lava-fountaining that form cinder cones and spatter cones at the vent.
3. Cinder cones aren't famous as their eruptions usually don't cause any loss of life. Cinder cones grow rapidly and soon approach their maximum sizes. They rarely exceed 250m in height and 500m in diameter.
4. When hot erupting lava contains just enough explosive gas to prevent the formation of a lava-flow, but not enough to shatter it into small fragments, the lava is torn by expanding gases into fluid hot clots, ranging in sizes from 1cm to 50cm across. Such volcanoes are called spatter volcanoes.
5. A volcano that consists of a complex of two or more vents is known as a compound or complex volcano.

BITS OF FACT

The largest volcano is Mauna Loa, in Hawaii. The tallest volcano is Mauna Kea, which, when measured from its base on the ocean floor, is more than 30,000 feet high.

WHAT DO YOU KNOW ABOUT THE THEORY OF THE MOVEMENT OF THE EARTH'S PLATES?

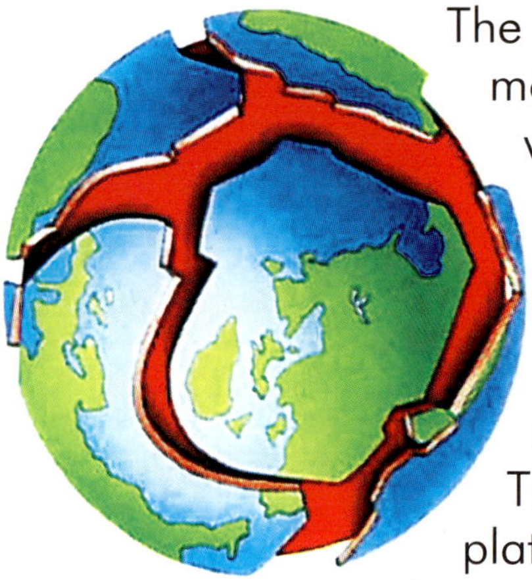

The theory of plate tectonics explains the movement of the Earth's plates. This theory was developed in the 1960's. This theory explains the movement of the Earth's plates and also explains the cause of earthquakes, volcanoes, oceanic trenches, the formation of mountain range and other geologic phenomena. The Earth's crust is divided into huge, thick plates that drift atop the soft mantle also. The plates are made of rock and are about 80 to 400 miles (50 to 250 km) thick. They move both horizontally and vertically. Over long periods of time, the plates also change in sizes as their margins are added to, crushed together or pushed back into the Earth's mantle. The plates are moving at a speed that has been estimated at 1 to 10 cm per year. Most of the Earth's seismic activities (volcanos and earthquakes) occur at the plate boundaries as they interact. The top layers of the plates are called the crust. Oceanic crust (the crust under the oceans) is thinner and denser than continental crust. Oceanic crust is more active than continental crust. Crust is constantly being created and destroyed.

BITS OF FACT

At the boundaries of the plates, various deformations occur as the plates interact; they separate from one another (the seafloor spreads), collide (forming mountain ranges), slip past one another (subduction zones in which plates undergo destruction and remelting) and slip laterally.

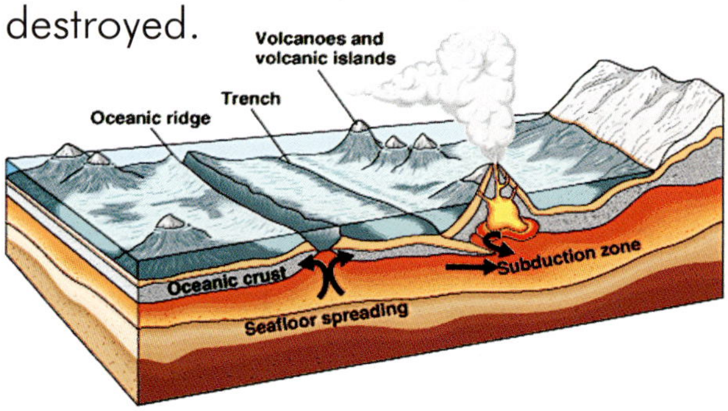

WHAT DO YOU KNOW ABOUT RIVER HWANG HO?

Hwang Ho is the muddiest river in the world. It flows in China. It carries so much silt that you could use to build a vast wall 40m (131ft) high and 6 m (20ft) wide all round the world. River Hwang Ho is also known as Yellow River. It is the second-longest river in China after River Yangtze. It originates from the Bayankala Mountains in Qinghai Province in western China; it flows through the nine provinces of China and empties into the Bohai Sea. The river gets its yellow colour mostly from the fine-grained calcareous silts which originates at the Loess Plateau and are carried in the flow. Silt deposition and diking over the centuries have caused the river to flow above the surrounding farmland, making flooding a critically dangerous problem. River Yellow carries 1.6 billion tons of silt annually at the point where it descends from the Loess Plateau. Due to its heavy load of silt, River Yellow is a depositing stream, that is, it deposits the part of its carried burden of soil in its bed in stretches where it is flowing slowly. These deposits elevate the riverbed which flows between natural levees in its lower reaches.

BITS OF FACT

Chinese Civilization is believed to have originated in the Yellow River Basin. Therefore it is considered as "The Mother River" and "The Cradle of the Chinese Civilization". Its nicknames are both "China's pride" and "China's sorrow".

WHAT DO YOU KNOW ABOUT THE GREAT SPHINX OF GIZA?

The Great Sphinx of Giza is the largest structure created from a single piece of stone. It stands at 66.34 ft (20.22 m) high. It is 241 ft (73.5 m) long and 20 ft (6 m) wide. The Great Sphinx of Giza is a half-human, half-lion statue located in Egypt, on the Giza Plateau at the west bank of River Nile, near modern day Cairo. The commonly held belief is that it was created during the 2700s B.C. Most of the pyramids were believed to have been created at the will of King Khafra whose pyramid happens to be situated there. Some Egyptologists are of the opinion that the Great Sphinx represents the likeness of King Khafra who is often credited as its builder as well. The time of its construction is speculated to have been somewhere between 2520 B.C. and 2494 B.C. Because the limited evidence giving the origins of Khafra is ambiguous and circumstantial, the idea of the builder of the Sphinx and the exact date of its construction continue to be the subject of debate. The material of the Sphinx is the limestone bedrock, which originated fifty million years ago from the sediments deposited at the bottom of sea waters that engulfed northeast Africa during the Middle Eocene period.

BITS OF FACT

The Great Pyramid at Giza in Egypt, constructed around 2500 B.C., was the tallest building in the world until the Lincoln Cathedral was erected in 1311. All of the significant major pyramids were built over a time period of about 200 years.

WHAT DO YOU KNOW ABOUT SOUND WAVES?

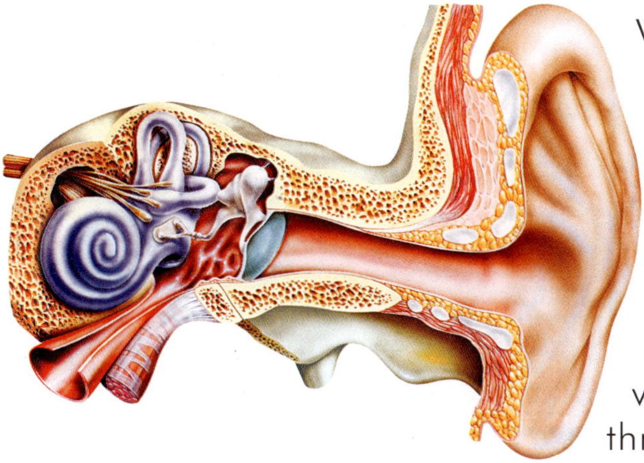

Various kinds of sounds which we hear, from a whisper to a roar, are nothing but simply moving air. When a sound is made, it causes vibrations in the air. These vibrations carry the sound to our ears. The vibrations that carry sound through the air are called sound waves. In other words, sound is the transfer of energy in the form of waves. The waves travel by bumping air molecules together. The air molecules move back and forth, but the wave of energy moves outwards. The speed with which the waves travel through air depend solely on temperature. Sound waves travel faster through solids and liquids rather than through air. The reason behind this is that the molecules are densely packed together in liquids and solids. There is complete silence in space because there are no molecules to carry the sound waves. Sound travels with a speed of about 344 m/s in air at 20 degrees Centigrade. It travels faster in warm air reaching the speed of about 386 m/s at 100 degrees Centigrade. It travels at 1500 m/s in water.

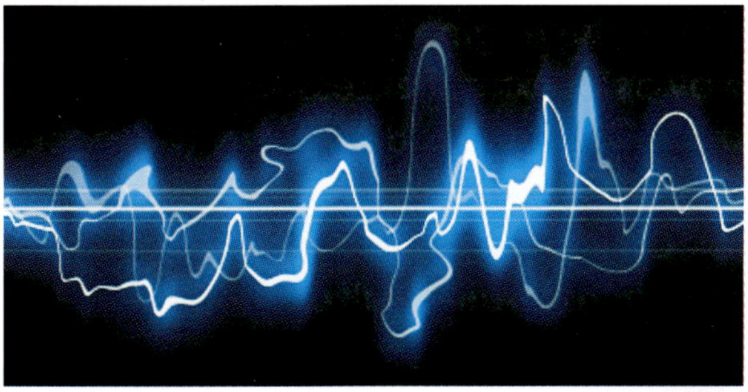

BITS OF FACT

Light travels a million times faster than sound. That is why we see a flash of lightning before we hear thunder, even though both occur at the same time.

WHAT DO YOU KNOW ABOUT THE JET OPERATING DURING BAD WEATHER CONDITIONS?

A jet flies by gathering quickmoving air in its inlets. The incoming air is squeezed in with the help of rotary fans. Fuel is squirted into the compressed air which burns the mixture. As a result, the hot, burnt gases are pushed towards the back and the jet moves forwards.

Intense rain or hail may cause the combustor to burn the air-fuel mixture less efficiently. Usually, this effect is negligible because the intense period of a storm is generally brief. Normal rain, hail or snowstorms do not produce enough water. Even if they do so, the high temperatures in the combustion chamber evaporate the moisture. The water only adds a slight amount of steam to the burning air-fuel mixture and doesn't reduce the engine power apparently. Furthermore, the engine is designed in such a way as to extract excessive water, snow or hail from the air before it reaches the combustion chamber. This is how a jet continues to function with snow, hail, or rain falling all around it.

BITS OF FACT

Hans von Ohain is considered to be the designer of the first operational turbojet engine. The was the first to register a patent for the turbojet engine in 1930. Hans von Ohain was granted a patent for his turbojet engine in 1936. However, Hans von Ohain's jet was the first to fly in 1939.

WHAT DO YOU KNOW ABOUT PHOTO GREY SUNGLASSES?

When you look at the photogrey sunglasses, they're as clear as glass. As you step outside in the sun, the glasses darken and block up to 80 per cent of the light radiation within a minute. Isn't it surprising? The sunglasses can change colours under light (photochromic material) because of a special manufacturing process. When the glass is molten, the tiny, transparent crystals of silver halide are added to it. The silver-halide crystals change chemically when the substantial amounts of ultraviolet light hit the glasses. The silver ions in the crystals combine with an electron to form silver atoms inside the glass. The silver blocks light and the glasses darken. The stronger the ultraviolet, the darker the grey. Halogen gas which is released when the silver ions formed atoms cannot escape the glass. When you remove the glasses by stepping inside, the trapped halogen gas atoms recombine with the silver atoms and form clear silver-halide crystals once more. The dark glass clears and becomes transparent again.

BITS OF FACT

Sunglasses or prescription eyeglasses that darken when exposed to the sun were first developed by Corning in the late 1960s and popularized by Transitions in the 1990s.

What do you know about Safety Glasses?

A safety glass is a type of glass that, when struck, breaks into tiny, relatively harmless fragments rather than shattering into large, harmful pieces. Safety glasses may be made in two ways. They may be constructed by laminating the two sheets of ordinary glass together with a thin interlayer of plastic. They may be produced by strengthening glass sheets by heat. Good quality safety glasses are made from polycarbonate and are shatter resistant. It doesn't mean that they are unbreakable or that they last for ever. Their purpose is to protect the wearer from an injury that may result due to accidental projectiles and particles. Although safety lenses may be constructed from a variety of materials of various impact resistances yet, certain standards suggest that they must maintain a minimum 1 millimetre thickness at the thinnest point. Safety glasses can vary in the level of protection they provide. The safety glasses used in a factory must have stronger lenses and a stronger frame with additional shields at the temples, whereas the safety glasses used while welding have much darker lenses.

BITS OF FACT

Polarized safety glasses feature polarized lens technology that reduces glare without sacrificing clarity, performance or durability. This feature eliminates eye stress and fatigue from any surfaces that create glare, *i.e.* from sunlight, water, sand, snow, glass and chrome.

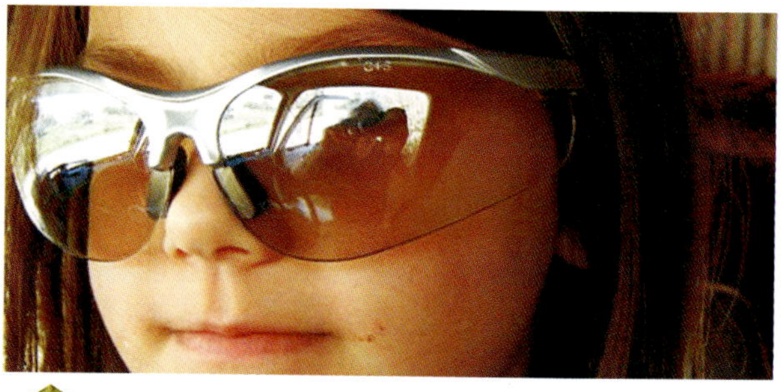

WHAT DO YOU KNOW ABOUT THE VARIOUS USES OF WAX?

Waxes may be natural and artificial. Natural wax is a substance that is secreted by bees and used by them in constructing their honeycombs. In addition to beeswax, carnauba (epicuticular wax of a plant) and paraffin (a petroleum wax) are waxes which occur naturally. Artificial waxes are esters. It means that they are the combinations of long chain of alcohols and long chain of fatty acids. Wax is used in several ways:-

1. As a water-resistant coating on cars and furniture.
2. They are used in lipsticks and eyebrow pencils, in liquid soaps and shampoos to give a pearl-essence effect.
3. Lanolin is a wax made by sebaceous glands of sheep. It is washed out of wool with detergents. It is used in many hair and skincare products.
4. Waxes are made into candles, but most candles these days are made from a long chain of hydrocarbons (called paraffin) which are not true waxes.
5. Waxes are the principal component in traditional varnishes such as shellac.

BITS OF FACT

AutoGuard Wax is a waterless cleaner/wax that contains both carnuaba and montan waxes which give your vehicle a hard, glossy, long-lasting shine.

WHAT DO YOU KNOW ABOUT MAGNETS?

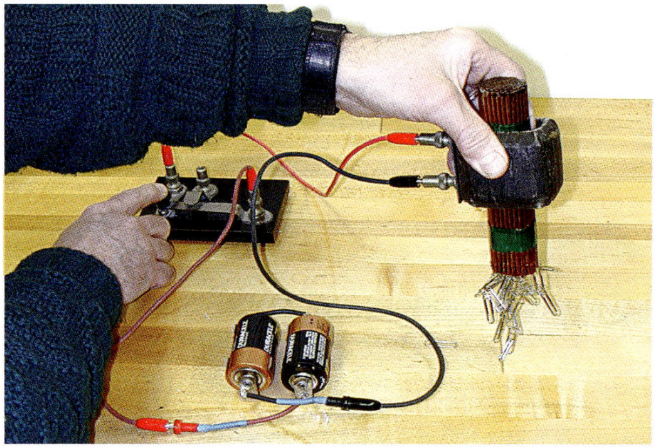

We observe that when a metal object is brought close to a magnet, it gets attracted and sticks onto it. This happens because when a metal object is brought close to a magnet, it makes a line of force. This line of force is not visible to the human eye, but it can be felt by a simple experiment. If we put iron particles on a thin piece of paper and put that paper on the magnet, the iron particles will fall exactly in the area of the line of force. This line of force is known as the "magnetic field". The points at which the iron particles are attracted to the magnet are known as the magnetic poles. All magnets have two ends, usually marked "north" and "south". The fundamental law of all magnets is: Opposites attract and likes repel. So, if you have two bar magnets with their ends marked "north" and "south," the north end of one magnet will attract the south end of the other. On the other hand, the north end of one magnet will repel the north end of the other.

BITS OF FACT

The most famous magnetic magic of all is the Aurora Borealis or the Northern Lights. Under specific conditions, at the ends of the earth's magnetic field, one can observe the solar winds passing overhead in a brilliant display of color and light. Records have shown that people and perhaps even small villages have been sucked up into space by these amazingly beautifully unbelievably powerful natural phenomena.

WHAT DO YOU KNOW ABOUT THE WORKING OF AN ELECTRIC TOASTER?

An electric toaster changes electrical energy to heat energy. Inside the appliance are the loops of special mixture of metals. Nichrome, a nickel-chromium alloy, is one of them. Electricity cannot pass through this special metal very easily. The metal slows down the electrons and holds up the current flowing through it. This is called the "resistance" of the metal. When the resistance of a metal is higher, the metal gets hot because of the friction of the electrons in the current of electricity. As the electricity is forced through the wires, the wires begin to heat up and glow very hot causing the bread to become brown. At the same time, a bimetallic strip heats and expands. One of the two metals in this strip expands more quickly than the other causing the strip to curve. As it bends, it completes an electrical circuit and activates an electromagnet. The magnet attracts a catch and releases the spring that holds the racks in the toaster. The elements switch off and the toasted slices pop up.

BITS OF FACT

In 1946, an engineer named Percy Spencer was experimenting with a magnetron tube (a tube which forms microwaves). Later on, he saw that the candy bar in his pocket had melted. This puzzled him, so he tried an experiment. This time, he put some popcorn kernels beside the magnetron tube. Soon, the whole laboratory was full of popping popcorn. In this way, the first microwave oven was invented.

WHAT DO YOU KNOW ABOUT THERMOMETERS?

A thermometer is a device that measures the temperature of a person's body, the air etc. The name is made up of two smaller words: "thermo" means heat and "meter" means to measure. There is usually a bulb at the base of the thermometer with a long glass tube stretching out to the top. Early thermometers used water. As water froze, there was no way to measure temperatures less than the freezing point of water. So, alcohol, which freezes at temperature below the point where water freezes, was used. The red coloured or silver line in the middle of the thermometer moves up and down depending on the temperature. When you look at a thermometer, you'll see a thin red or silver line that grows longer when it is hotter. The line goes down in cold weather. This liquid is sometimes coloured alcohol but can also be a metallic liquid called mercury. Both mercury and alcohol grow bigger when heated, whereas they grow smaller when cooled. Numbers are placed alongside the glass tube that mark the temperature when the line is at that point.

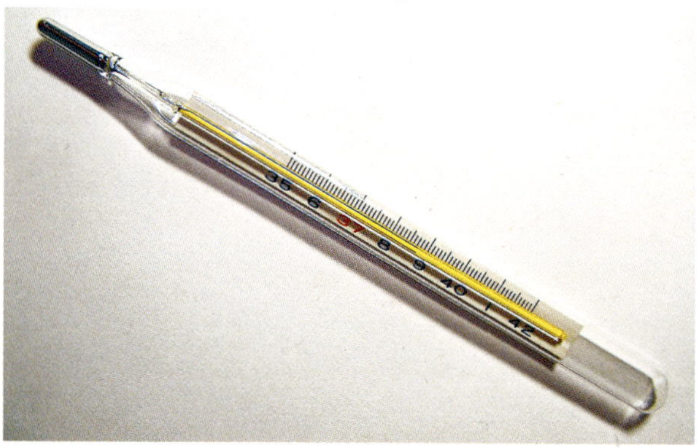

BITS OF FACT

The inventor of the first thermometer is thought to have been a very famous Italian scientist called Galileo Galilei. His thermometer had one end open. The first "closed" thermometer was invented by Ferdinando II, Grand Duke of Tuscany in, 1654.

What do you know about a chemical reaction?

A chemical reaction is a process wherein the chemical properties of a substance are altered by the rearrangement of the atoms in the substance. A chemical reaction occurs when bonds between atoms are made or broken. There are different types of chemical reactions.

When wood burns in the presence of oxygen, it is turned to ash. It becomes an entirely different mixture than it was before. Obviously, the ashes cannot be simply frozen to turn them back into wood again. This is an example of an irreversible chemical reaction. Chemical reactions may also involve changes in colour. In specific proportions and under the right conditions, carbon which is black can be combined with colourless hydrogen and oxygen to produce white sugar. Chemical reactions which give off heat are called exothermic reactions. The speeds of reactions are determined by factors like temperatures around and the sizes and shapes of reactants.

BITS OF FACT

The rusting of a steel garbage-can is a chemical reaction. Rusting happens because the iron (Fe) in the metal combines with oxygen (O_2) in the atmosphere. If you put pure hydrogen gas (H_2) and pure oxygen gas in a room, they can be involved in a reaction.

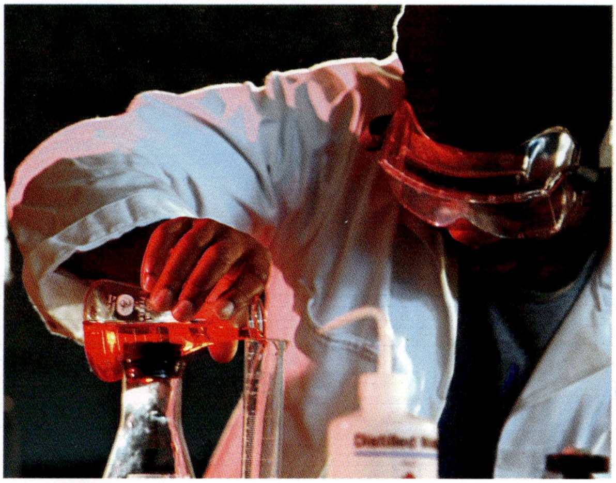

WHAT DO YOU KNOW ABOUT THE TRANSFER OF ENERGY?

Anything which happens from the drop of a pin to an explosion requires energy. Energy is defined as the ability to put effort and enthusiasm into a piece of work and work is defined as the use of energy to do work. There are various forms of energy like heat, light, sound, electrical, chemical, nuclear, potential and kinetic energies. The Law of the Conservation of energy states that the total amount of energy in the Universe is fixed. Energy can neither be created nor destroyed; it can only be transferred or changed into one form or another. For example, an object gains potential energy when it is lifted. As soon as the object is released, potential energy is transferred into the energy of motion or kinetic energy. During this transference, some of the energy is converted into heat energy.

BITS OF FACT

The amount of energy produced by the Sun in a 2-week period equals the combined stored energy of all the coal, iron and natural gas reserves known to man.

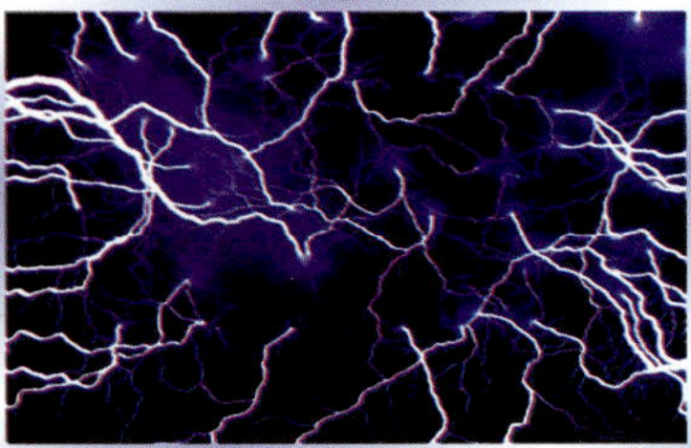

WHAT DO YOU KNOW ABOUT FORCE?

Force is a push or pull exerted upon an object due to its interaction with another object. Whenever there is an interaction between two objects, there is a force upon each of the objects. In other words, in order to make a stationary object move or a moving object stop, force is required. There are various types of forces. For simplicity, all forces are divided into two groups - contact forces and action-at-a-distance forces. Contact forces are types of forces in which the two interacting objects are physically in contact with each other. Action-at-a-distance forces are types of forces in which the two interacting objects are not in physical contact with each other. Still, they are able to exert a push or pull. Examples of action-at-a-distance forces include gravitational forces (e.g., the sun and planets exert a gravitational pull on each other in spite of their large separation) and magnetic forces (e.g., two magnets can exert a magnetic pull on each other even when separated by a distance of a few centimetres).

BITS OF FACT

The air resistance is a special type of frictional force which acts upon objects as they travel through the air. It is most noticeable for persons who travel at high speeds (e.g., a skydiver or a downhill skier) or for objects with large surface areas.

What do you know about remote controls?

A remote control is an electronic device used for the remote operation of a machine. Remote controls are used to issue commands from a distance to televisions or other consumer electronics such as stereo systems and DVD players. They are usually small wireless hand-held objects with a number of buttons for adjusting various settings such as surfing television channels, tracking numbers and the adjustment of volume. A remote control for an electronic appliance uses an infrared to emit a beam of light that reaches the device. This light is invisible to the human eye but carries signals that are detected by the appliance. When a person presses a button on his/her remote control, it tells a tiny computer processor to trigger a light emitting device called a diode which is located at the front of the remote. The diode, then, sends an infrared signal to a light sensitive area called photocell on the person's T.V. set. These light signals are repeated five times a second.

BITS OF FACT

The first TV remote control, called "Lazy Bones", was developed in 1950 by Zenith Electronics Corporation. The infrared remote technologies were invented in the 1980s.

What do you know about a CD?

Basically, a Compact Disc(CD) is nothing more than a plastic (polycarbonate) disc with several layers. It is principally made up of injection-moulded polycarbo-nate. The diameter of a CD is about 12 cm and is about 1.2 mm thin. A CD has a track of tiny pits in a silvery reflective layer on a plastic disc. It is read by a laser which enters the CD on the play side, travels through the CD's clear plastic layer and picks up information from the layer data on the silvery surface between the pits. Then, the laser bounces off the reflective coating on the back side of the data layer. The reflected laser beam, then, travels back through the clear plastic layer, out of the CD, and into the "detector" of the CD player. As the CD rotates, the information is translated into a sequence of signals. These signals are interpreted by the detector as strings of zeros and ones.

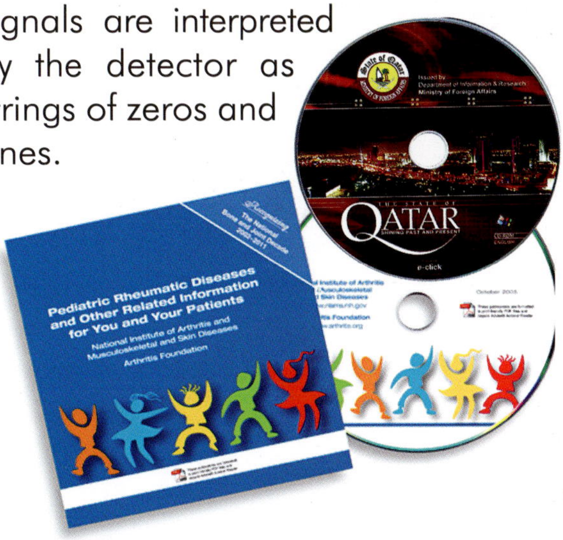

BITS OF FACT

Most CDs can hold up to 2,50,000 pages of typed text. The CD was developed by Philips and Sony in 1980.

WHAT DO YOU KNOW ABOUT FLYING KITES?

The basic principle of flying a kite has to do with a difference in air pressure. When air moves quickly over a surface, the pressure is decreased. When air moves more slowly, the pressure is increased. A kite flies because it deflects the wind downwards and the resulting change in momentum produces an upward force. The reason for this is that the air travelling over the top of the curved surface of the kite is going faster than the air passing underneath. Fast-moving air creates less pressure; this means there is more pressure underneath the kite. This helps to force it upwards. The kite string keeps the kite at an angle of attack to the wind. The wind hits the kite and flows down the path of least resistance. The air exerts an equal and opposite upward force on the kite and the kite rises due to this lift. In other words, the kite blocks the wind. Then, the kite pushes down on the air. Finally, the air pushes back up on the kite and lifts it into the sky.

BITS OF FACT

The record for the highest single kite flown is 3,801 metres (12,471ft) and for a train of kites 9,740 metres (31,955 ft). The largest number of kites flown on a single line is 11,284. This record is held by a Japanese kite maker.

WHAT DO YOU KNOW ABOUT THE FIRST METAL BRIDGE?

The world's first cast iron bridge was built over River Severn in Coalbrook-dale, Shropshire, in 1779.

It was the first bridge ever to be built of iron. It is perhaps the most important industrial monument in Britain.

It attracted visitors from all over the world. The bridge was designed by Thomas Pritchard and built by Abraham Darby. The technique of smelting iron with coke was perfected by Abraham Darby, who used the product to build the bridge. As soon as the bridge was built, a community started to form around it and the town of Ironbridge was born. The semicircular arch of the bridge spans 100.5 feet (30.6 m) and has five arch ribs, each cast in two halves. All the major parts were put together in three months without a single accident or the least obstruction to the boats in the river. It was the industrial revolution which brought about the beginning of metal bridges. Previously, bridges were constructed of stone and timber.

BITS OF FACT

A suspension bridge is a bridge with its deck supported by large cables hung from towers. The world's longest suspension bridge is the Akashi Kaikyo Bridge in Japan. It is a huge three-span cable-stayed bridge some 3910 metres in total length with a centre span of 1990 metres.

WHAT DO YOU KNOW ABOUT THE SUBMARINE?

A submarine is a watercraft that can operate underwater. It ranges from a two-man vessel, which can examine the sea floor for a few hours to the Russian Typhoon class, which can remain submerged for 6 months and carry nuclear missiles capable of destroying multiple cities.

William Bourne, a British mathematician, drew plans for a submarine in 1578. It was only in 1620 that Cornelius van Drebbel, a Dutch inventor, managed to build a submarine. He wrapped a wooden rowboat tightly in waterproofed leather and had air tubes with floats to the surface to provide oxygen. He took the first trip with 12 oarsmen in River Thames and stayed submerged for 3 hours. The first submarine used for military purposes was built in 1776 by David Bushnell of the US. His "Turtle" was a one man, wooden submarine powered by hand turned propellers. It was used during the American Revolution against British warships. The Turtle would approach the enemy ship partially submerged to attach explosives to the hull of the enemy ship.

BITS OF FACT

While the largest submarines stretch up to almost 200 metres, the smallest working submarine, the *Water Beetle*, is only 2.7 metres long. It can go down to 30 metres and stay underwater for four hours.

WHAT DO YOU KNOW ABOUT THE LARGEST BATTLESHIP EVER BUILT?

A battleship is a large, heavily armoured warship with a main battery consisting of the largest calibre of guns. Battleships were larger, better armed and better armoured than cruisers and destroyers. The last battleships were withdrawn from service in 2006. Yamato, the largest battleship ever built, was named after the ancient Japanese Yamato Province. It was a battleship of the Imperial Japanese Navy during World War II. The design of this super battleship (class of warships) was initiated by Japan's Naval General Staff in 1934. The construction of the Yamato began after the Japanese had withdrawn from the Washington Naval Treaty at the Second London Conference of 1936. It had nine 460mm (18.1-inch) main battery guns which fired 1460kg (3,200 pounds) armour piercing shells. These guns were the largest battleship guns ever to go to the sea. The Yamato was completed soon after the Japanese attack on the U.S. base at Pearl Harbor on 7th December 1941. It was a huge battleship. It had 200,000 horsepower turbines which gave it a top speed of 31 knots and a range of 7,200 miles. It hosted a crew of 2,747 officers and men.

BITS OF FACT

The American Texas (1912) is the only preserved example of a Dreadnought-type battleship that dates to the time of the original HMS Dreadnought.

WHAT DO YOU KNOW ABOUT WEATHER SATELLITES?

A weather satellite is a type of satellite that is primarily used to monitor the weather and climate of the Earth. The first weather satellite, Vanguard 2, was launched on 17th February 1959. It was designed to measure cloud cover and resistance, but the poor axis of rotation kept it from collecting a notable amount of useful data. The first weather satellite to be considered a success was TIROS-1, launched by NASA on 1st April, 1960. This marked the first day when it became possible to observe the Earth's weather conditions on a regular basis. The satellite designed to obtain the pictures of clouds was rocketed into space aboard a Thor-Able launch vehicle on 1st April, 1960, from Cape Canaveral, Florida. The satellite was basically a cylinder with 18 flattened sides to mount solar power cells. The satellite was approximately 42 inches in diameter, 22 inches high (including the projecting television camera lens) and had a launch weight of approximately 128.4kg including fuel for small solid rockets to control the spin-over time of the satellite . TIROS-I operated for 78 days.

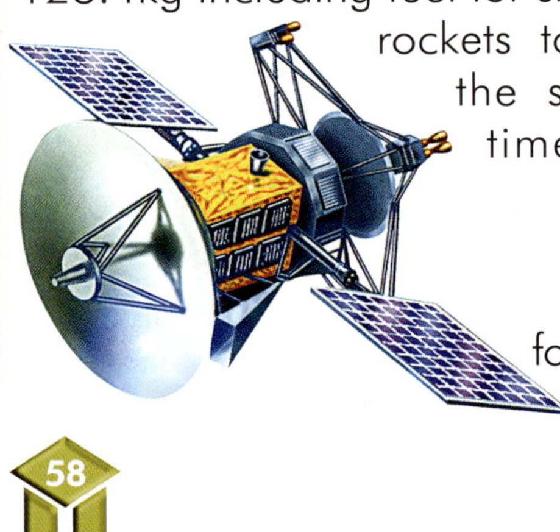

BITS OF FACT

There are over 2,500 satellites in orbit around the Earth. There are also over 10,000 man-made objects orbiting around the Earth.

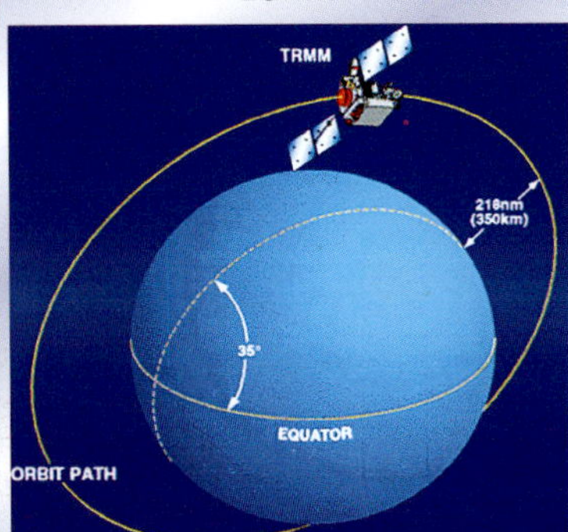

WHAT DO YOU KNOW ABOUT THE RIBS IN THE HUMAN BODY?

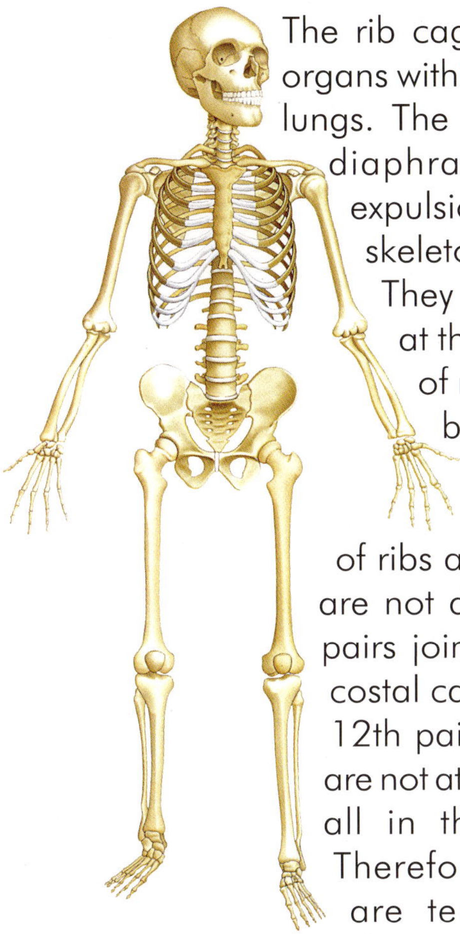

The rib cage is specially designed to protect the organs within the chest, especially the heart and the lungs. The movement of the rib cage assists the diaphragm in controlling the intake and expulsion of air during breathing. The human skeleton has 24 ribs arranged in 12 pairs. They join the thoracic vertebrae in the spine at the back. In the front, the first seven pairs of ribs are connected to the sternum or the breastbone directly by a costal cartilage hence, they are also referred to as "true ribs". The 8th, 9th and 10th pairs of ribs are also termed as "false ribs" since they are not directly attached to the sternum. These pairs join among themselves and then join the costal cartilage of the seventh rib. The 11th and 12th pairs of ribs are not attached at all in the front. Therefore, They are termed as "floating ribs".

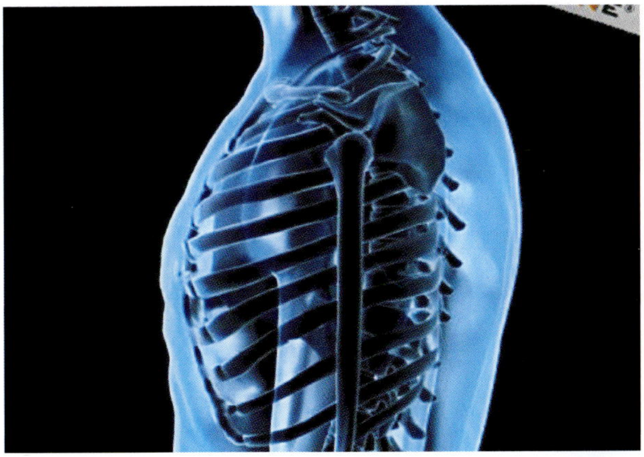

BITS OF FACT

If you sneeze too hard, you may fracture a rib. If you try to suppress your sneeze, you may rupture a blood vessel in your head and neck.

Every time your breathe, your ribs moves.

What do you know about the function of muscles in the body?

Muscles usually work in pairs. A muscle can only pull in one direction. So, it needs another muscle to pull in the opposite direction in order to return a bone to its original position. The best example of a pair of muscles working together can be seen in the human arm. The muscle at the front of the arm is called the biceps muscle. The muscle at the back of the arm is called the triceps muscle. When the biceps muscle is working (contracted), the triceps muscle is relaxed. When the triceps muscle is contracted, the biceps muscle is relaxed. This is called the antagonistic action of muscles because they are always working in opposite ways.

The contraction of the biceps muscle bends the arm.

The contraction of the triceps muscle straightens the arm. There are muscles in the legs which work in the same way to bend the knees, ankles and toes.

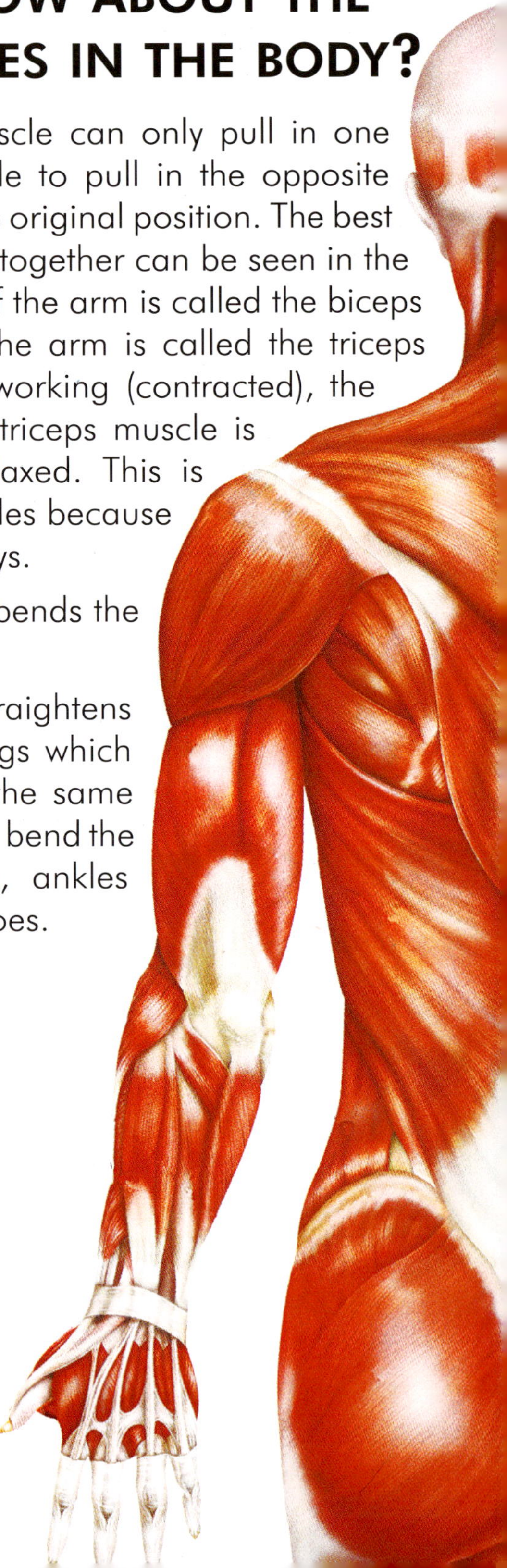

BITS OF FACT

Both the lion and the antelope have well-developed muscles in their limbs. They need to use them often. Arthropods also have muscles but we cannot see them because they are inside their hard body-coverings. These muscles also work in pairs as vertebrate muscles do.

What can you tell about chewing your food and breathing at the same time?

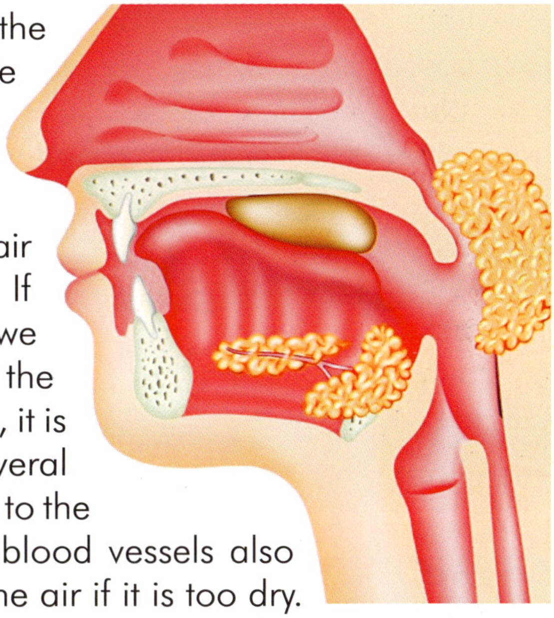

We can chew our food and breathe at the same time. This is possible because the nose is separated from the mouth by a bone called the palate. The nose is a biological air conditioning unit. It contains hair which traps large dust particles. If there is a lot of dust in the air, we may sneeze to remove it from the nostrils. If cold air enters the nose, it is warmed by the blood in the several capillaries, which are found close to the walls of the nasal cavity. These blood vessels also provide water which humidifies the air if it is too dry. We can feel the difference between cold and dry air which is breathed into the lungs via the nose and the same type of air breathed in via the mouth. The air, then, passes into the throat and down the windpipe (trachea). The entrance to the trachea is protected by a valve, the epiglottis, which closes when we swallow food or drink. In this way, the air passage is only blocked for a second. So we do not have to hold our breath.

BITS OF FACT

It is interesting to note that reptiles and amphibians do not have palates. So, when they eat something, they have to hold their breath.

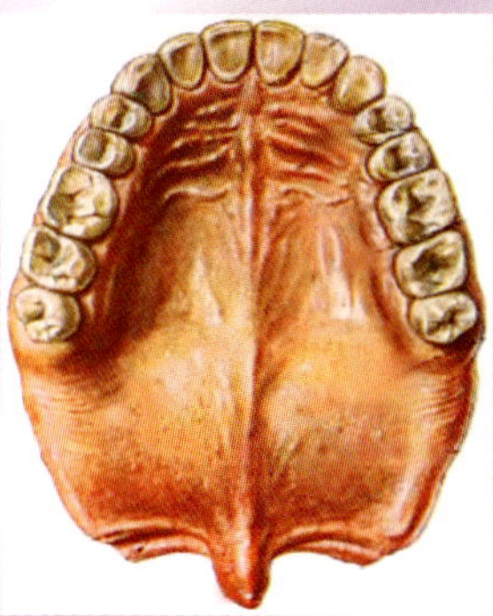

What do you know about nerve impulses?

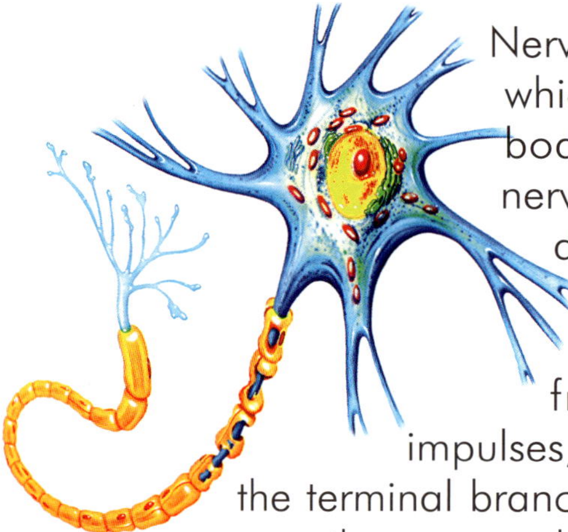

Nerve impulses are tiny electrical signals which travel through the nerve cells of the body and convey information. Each nerve cell has small projections called dendrites. These dendrites extend out from the cell body and are responsible for receiving messages from the other nerve cells. The impulses, then, travel down along the axon to the terminal branches. There, the impulses are carried across the gap to the next neuron by way of chemicals called neurotransmitters. These chemicals are capable of binding to the receptors found in the dendrites of the next receiving nerve cell. Once, a number of receptors on the receiving cell have chemicals bound to them, they trigger changes in the receiving neuron. This enables it to send the electrical signal down its axon. When the signal reaches the end of the axon, it again triggers the release of neurotransmitters that are, then, picked up by the next receiving nerve cell. This process is repeated over and over in rapid succession.

BITS OF FACT

Messages travel along the nerves as electrical impulses. They travel at speed of up to 248 miles per hour.

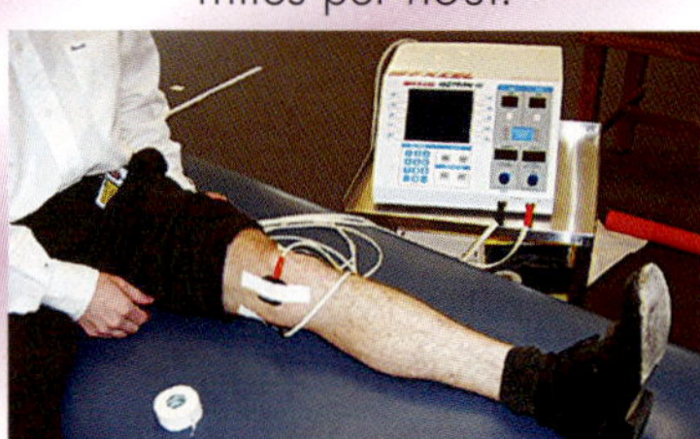

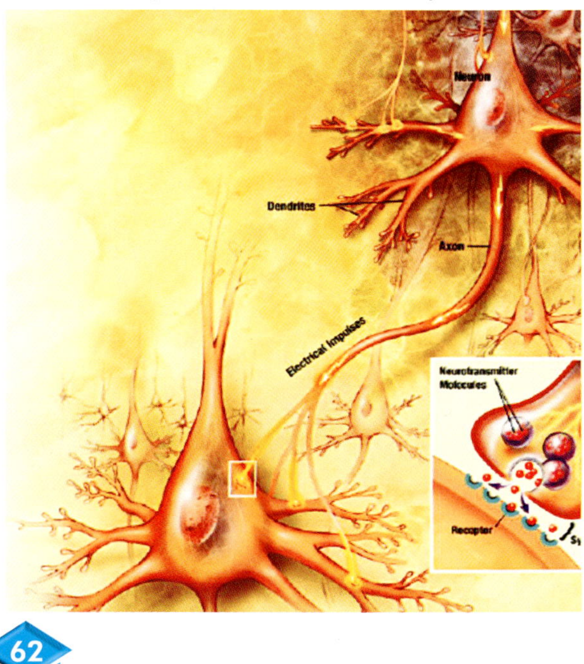

WHAT DO YOU KNOW ABOUT HICCUPS?

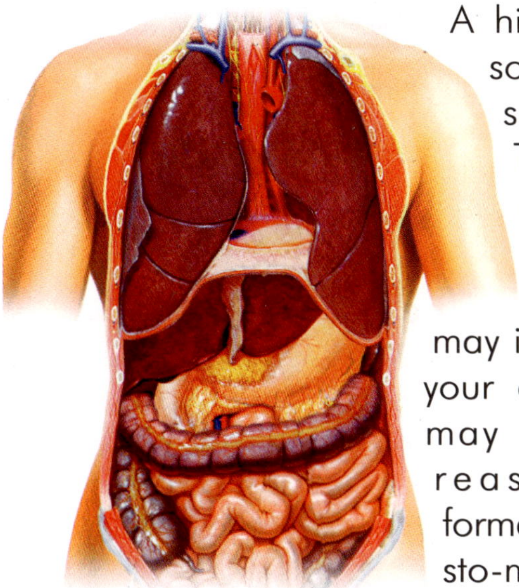

A hiccup is a sharp, usually repeated sound made in the throat. It is by a sudden movement of the diaphragm. This happens when you eat too much, drink bubbly drinks like soda or swallow too much air. When you eat very hot food, it may irritate a passage in your digestive system. It may even be the reason for the forma-tion of gas in the sto-mach. This gas presses against the diaphragm. The diaphragm is an organ which separates the chest from the stomach. It tightens up and pulls air into the lungs. Because it has tightened up, the air cannot get through all the way to the lungs. It is stopped short by the diaphragm. You feel a dump when this happens. This dumping feeling is described as hiccups. So, hiccups are a way of telling you that your body is trying to get rid of the hot food or gas in the stomach.

BITS OF FACT

It is not possible to tickle yourself. The cerebellum, a part of the brain, warns the rest of the brain that you are about to tickle yourself. Since your brain knows this, it ignores the resulting sensation.

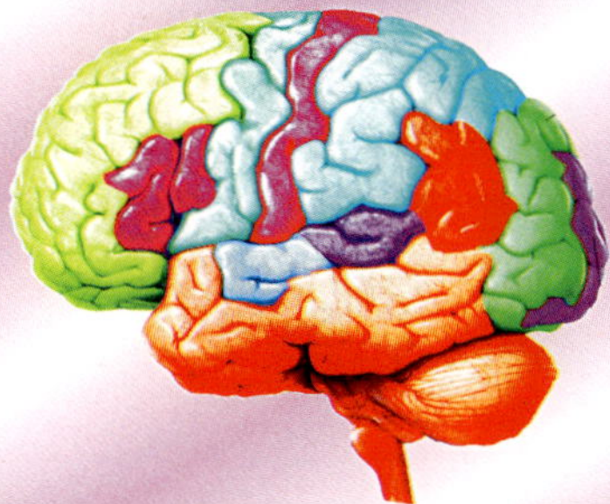

What do you know about the people being left-handed?

When a person is left-handed, it means that he/she can do certain things better with the left side of his/her body than with the right side. But the question arises as to how a person is left-handed. One theory rests on the centres of the two halves of the brain, *i.e.* the left half and the right half. It is believed that the left half of the brain predominates over the right half. This theory is based on the fact that the nerves from the brain cross over at neck-level to the opposite sides of the body. As a result, the opposite sides of the body are supplied by the opposite sides of the brain. The left half of the brain controls the right half of the body and renders it more skillful while reading, writing speaking, and working. It makes most people right-handed. On the other hand, it is just the reverse in case of a left handed person. The right half of the brain controls the left half of the brain and, hence, a person works best with the left side of his/her body.

BITS OF FACT

A human body is not symmetrical. It means that the right side is slightly different from the left side. For example, the right hand may be stronger than the left; the two feet may vary in size or even the legs may differ in strength. Many of the greatest geniuses, including Michelangelo and Leonardo da Vinci, were left-handed.

WHAT CAN YOU TELL ABOUT THE SMELLING OF FEET?

The foot odour results due to the sweat-eating bacteria. Your feet smell too bad because the bacteria become attracted to the sweat on your feet and start feeding on it. The excretion of the bacteria has a strong odour that causes your feet to smell bad. What makes the situation even worse are the shoes and socks which trap the sweat on your skin. Now, the bacteria have their favourite kind of environment which is dark and damp inside the shoes. You sweat all over your hands which have a comparable number of sweat glands but they do not stink. Why? The answer is your socks and shoes. The sweat your feet excrete can't easily escape into the air like the sweat your hands excrete – it all collects on your skin and in your socks. The bacteria love this dark, damp feast and have a sort of feeding frenzy. When you take off your shoes, the smell that hits you is all the excretion made by the bacteria. It is collected on your feet and in your socks and shoes. Some people's feet smell more than others' because of the simple reason that these people sweat more than others.

BITS OF FACT

Each foot has over 2,50,000 sweat glands in it and produces over a pint of sweat a day. It is a lot for bacteria to feed on.

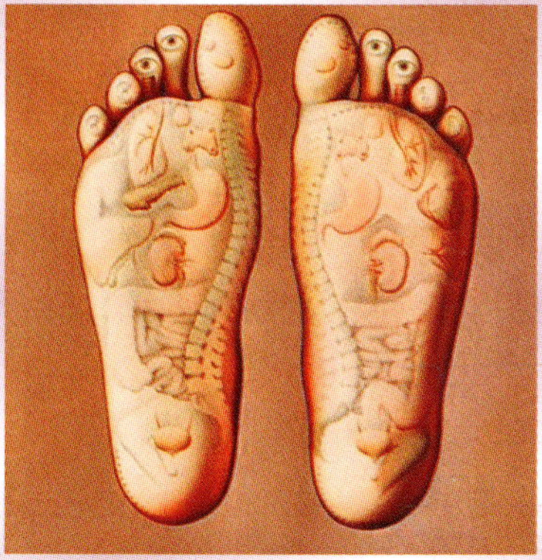

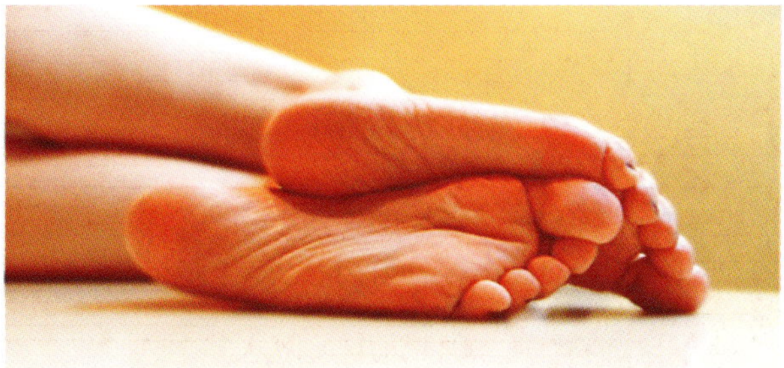

WHAT DO YOU KNOW ABOUT HEADACHES?

A headache is simply the painful symptom of an underlying disorder with multiple causes. There may be various causes for a headache, but it only indicates that there is a disorder somewhere in the body or in the nervous system. Common causes of a headache are tension, migraine, eye strain, dehydration, low blood-sugar and sinusitis. A headache does not mean that there is pain in the actual brain matter contained in the skull. It is actually the pain felt by the sensitive coverings of the brain, and of the large veins and arteries which drain fluid from the brain. Sinus, tooth, ear and muscle pain also produce headaches by radiating the pain to these sensitive coverings when they get tensed. Similarly, when the muscles spanning the neck and the base of the skull contract, headaches may occur. Another reason for headaches is when people experience the effects of sudden physical and emotional trauma.

BITS OF FACT

Adult women get headaches four times more often than men do. You can also get headaches after eating ice cream. This is caused by the spasms of a blood vessel. These spasms occur due to the intense cold from the ice cream. The spasms interrupt the blood flow and cause the vessels to swell.

What do you know about your eyebrows?

Except for showing that you are angry, your eyebrows do a lot to protect you. You do not know that. Well, it is true. The tiny, little line of hair above each of your eyes is called the eyebrow. It plays a very important role in keeping moisture out of your eyes. When it rains or when sweat drips down from the forehead, the eyebrows divert the flow of water or sweat away from your eyes to the side of your face. This keeps your eyes dry. The arch shape of the eyebrows enables you to see clearly while it is raining. Besides, it also keeps away perspiration from dripping into your eyes and causing irritation or burning sensation. Like your eyelashes, your eyebrows also protect you from dust and dirt. They trap dust and dirt and prevent them from entering your eyes. Eyebrows also act as one of your most expressive facial features. They help you to determine how people are feeling. If a person raises his/her eyebrows, chances are that he/she is surprised a bit.

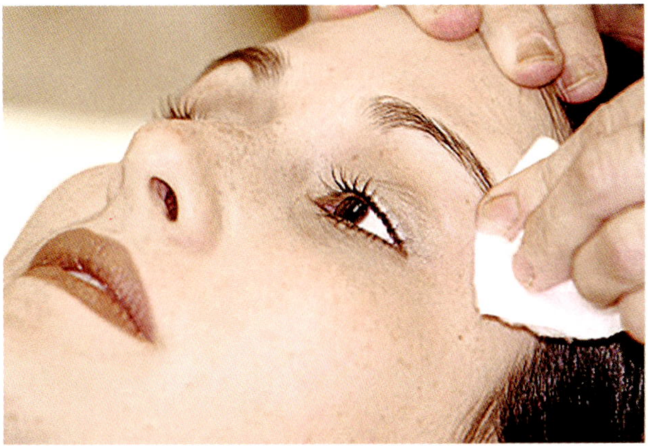

BITS OF FACT

There are approximately 550 hairs in an eyebrow.

WHAT DO YOU KNOW ABOUT YOUR REQUIREMENT OF SLEEP?

The amount of sleep an individual requires varies from person to person. On average, most adults need eight hours of sleep. Sleep plays an important role in our daily routine. During this inactive period, the body recharges the weary organs and tissues and brings back the energy required to start working effectively. The lifestyle of an individual is another factor in the amount of time he/she needs to regain his/her healthy balance and to feel fresh after he/she has got up. The quality of an individual's sleep is also another factor which determines the amount of sleep. The body rests during sleep. However, the brain remains active, gets "recharged" and still controls many bodily functions including breathing. Just like any other characteristics you are born with, the amount of sleep you need to function best may be different for you than for someone who is of the same age and gender. While you may be at your absolute best sleeping seven hours a night, someone else may clearly need nine hours to have a happy, productive life.

BITS OF FACT

Infants generally require about 16 hours a day of sleep, while teenagers need about 9 hours on average. For most adults, 7 to 8 hours at night is the best amount of sleep.

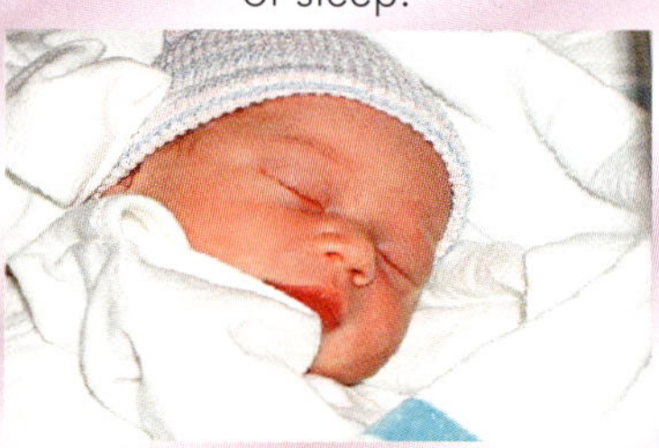

WHAT DO YOU KNOW ABOUT BAD BREATH?

According to the most current research, over 90 per cent of all the cases of chronic bad breath originate in the mouth, not in the stomach, sinuses or lungs. All the cases of bad breath are caused by Volatile Sulphur Compounds (VSCs). One compound is hydrogen sulphide (the rotten smell of an egg) and another is methyl mercaptan (the essence of skunk oil). The source of these compounds is bacteria in the mouth which break down the cell wall of dead cells. These anaerobic bacteria collect and multiply, mainly on the tongue. They thrive in a dry, dark environment such as under the gums, the spaces between the teeth and the crevices of the tongue. The diet of an individual can cause bad breath because certain foods increase the quantity of anaerobic bacteria that produce VSCs. It is believed that dieting can also cause bad breath.

BITS OF FACT

Coffee contains acids that decrease the oxygenation of the mouth, which, in turn, increases the production of bacteria. Dairy products are so high in proteins that the bacteria break down to create the VSCs. Mints and chewing gums which contain sugar, also produce VSCs when the anaerobic bacteria break them down.

WHAT CAN YOU SAY ABOUT SOME OF YOUR BODY PARTS 'FALLING ASLEEP'?

The unnerving, tingling sensation a person feels when his/her body part "falls asleep" is actually the result of nerves under pressure. For example, when a person sleeps in one position for a long time, his/her arm may fall asleep. This happens because the sleeping position exerts pressure on the nerves. As a result, the nerves carry the inhibited messages to the brain and to the rest of the body. At the same time, it also squeezes the blood vessels due to which the oxygen carried by these nerves never reaches its destination. When the sleeping position is changed, pressure from these nerves and blood vessels is released. The nerve fibres awaken in order of their thickness, the thickest ones awaken the last. This awakening process causes the different sensations (first tingling and then burning) a person experiences, as his/her affected body-parts return to normal.

BITS OF FACT

The nerves comprise the bundles of single-celled fibres, with each fibre conveying a different sensation or message to the brain. The fibres vary in thickness and in the amounts of myelin, a protective sheath which surrounds them. These two variables determine the sensitivity of the nerve fibre to pressure and to oxygen deprivation. As a general rule, the thicker the fibre, and the larger the myelin sheath, the more sensitive it is.

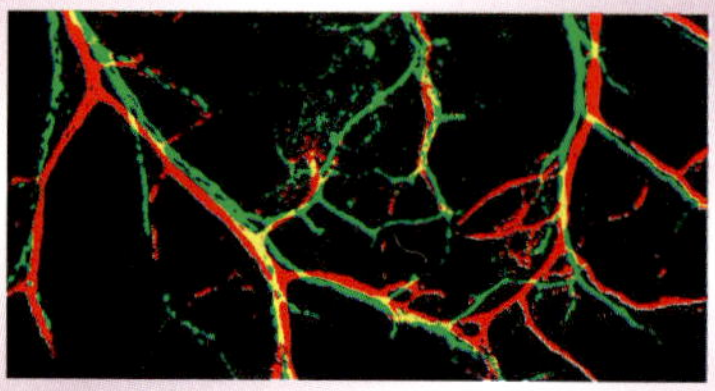

WHAT CAN YOU SAY ABOUT THE POPPING SOUND MADE BY THE JOINTS OF THE BODY?

When a person does a deep knee-bend, it is very likely that he/she hears a popping sound coming from the knee joints. Similarly, when he/she cracks his/her knuckles, he/she can also hear the popping sound. The question arises as to how we hear these popping sounds?

The sound heard when a person does a deep knee-bend is actually a snapping sound produced when his/her tendons (fibres that connect muscles and bones) elastically snap into new positions. As a result,his/her joints move under stress. Due to this back- and-forth movement of the tendon with the joint, he/she is able to hear the popping sound. Similarly, the sound heard, when a person's knuckles crack, results when a finger joint is extended almost to the end of its range. The joint, surrounded by a lubricating fluid, is encased in a capsule. The gas dissolved in the fluid separates from the solution and forms a small bubble. Thus, it makes a cracking sound.

BITS OF FACT

Ball and socket joints, like your hip and shoulder joints, are the most mobile of all joints. They allow you to swing your arms and legs in many different directions.

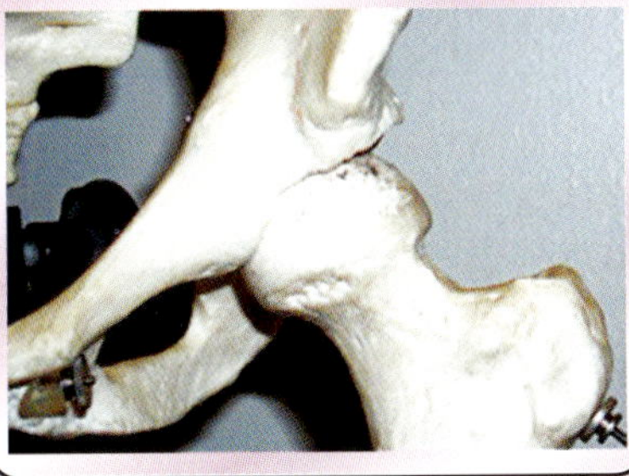

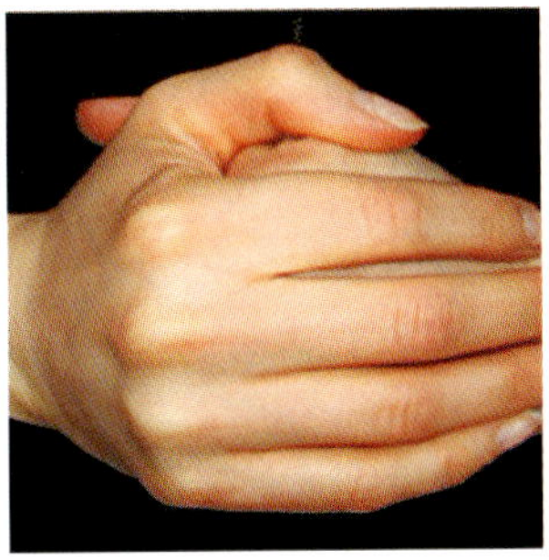

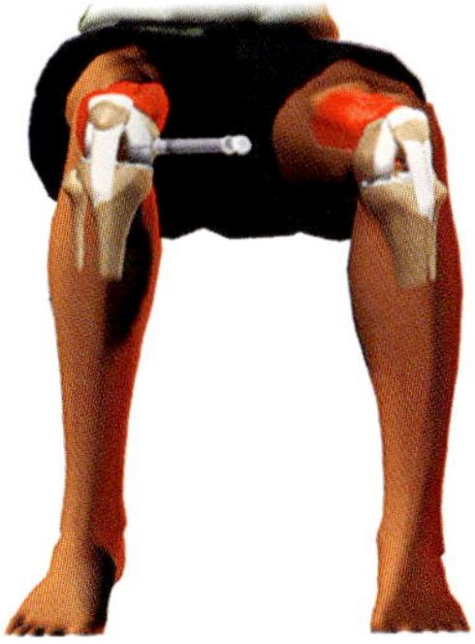

WHAT DO YOU KNOW ABOUT THE CELLS IN THE HUMAN BODY?

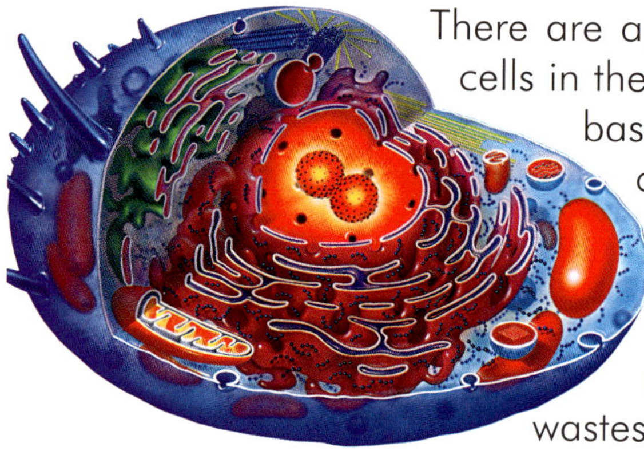

There are approximately 60 to 100 trillion cells in the body. A cell is one of the most basic units of life. It has a 'skin', called the plasma membrane which protects it from the outside environment. The cell membrane regulates the movement of water, nutrients and wastes into and out of the cell. Inside the cell membrane are the working parts of the cell. At the centre of the cell is the nucleus. The nucleus contains the DNA, the genetic code that co-ordinates protein synthesis. Besides, there are many organelles inside the cell – small structures that help carry out the day-to-day operations of the cell. One important cellular organelle is the ribosome. Ribosomes participate in protein synthesis. Another important cellular organelles are the mitochondria. They are often referred to as the power plants of the cell because many of the reactions that produce energy take place in mitochondria. Also important in the life of a cell are the lysosomes. Lysosomes are organelles that contain enzymes that aid in the digestion of nutrient molecules and other materials.

BITS OF FACT

On average, a cell measures 0.005mm in diameter. Large ones can measure as much as 0.02mm in diameter. A nerve cell can be up to 1 metre long.

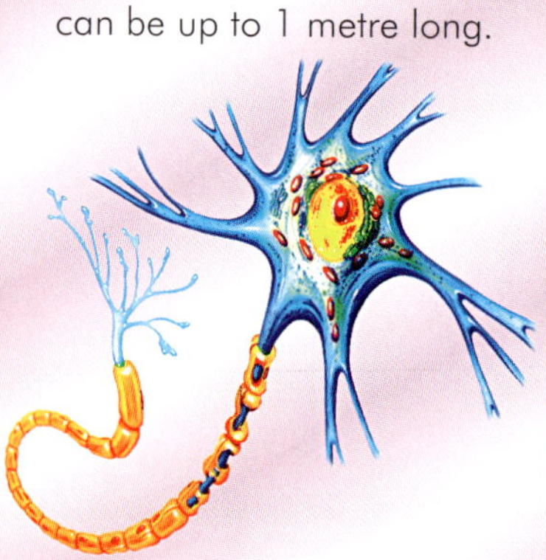

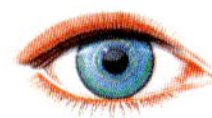

WHAT DO YOU KNOW ABOUT THE BASIC UNIT OF THE BRAIN?

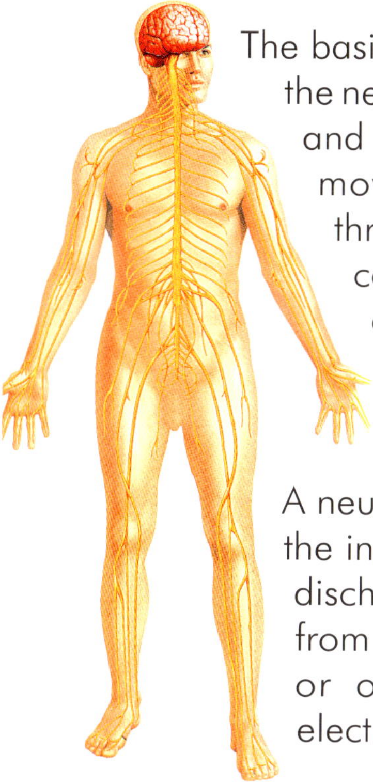

The basic computational unit in the nervous system is the nerve cell or neuron. Neurons transmit electrical and chemical signals that instruct the muscles to move. Nerve cells connect to one another through the spiny passages. Each of the nerve cells has three parts. The long arms of the nerve cell are axons. The "fingers" of the axons are called dendrites. At the end of dendrites are synapses. All of these parts of the nerve cell work together to connect cells to one another. A neuron receives input from other neurons. Once the input has exceeded a critical level, the neuron discharges a spike - an electrical pulse that travels from the body, down the axon, to the next neuron(s) or other receptors. The transmission of an electrical signal from one neuron to the next is effected by neuro-transmittors, chemicals which are released from the first neuron and bind themselves to the receptors in the second neuron. This link is called a synapse. The extent to which the signal from one neuron is passed on to the next depends on many factors, e.g. the amount of neurotransmittor available, the number and arrangement of receptors, amount of neuro-transmittor reabsorbed etc.

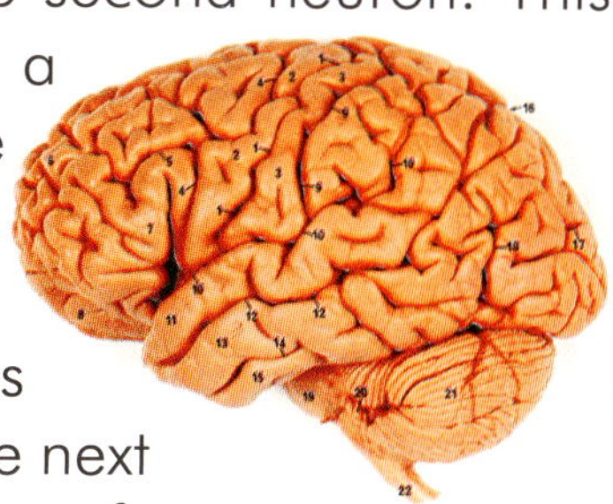

BITS OF FACT

At birth, the human brain contains its maximum number of neurons from 20 billion to 200 billion. Each neuron has 1,000 to 10,000 synapses or connections. The capacity of these neurons gives the brain a capacity to remember and think.

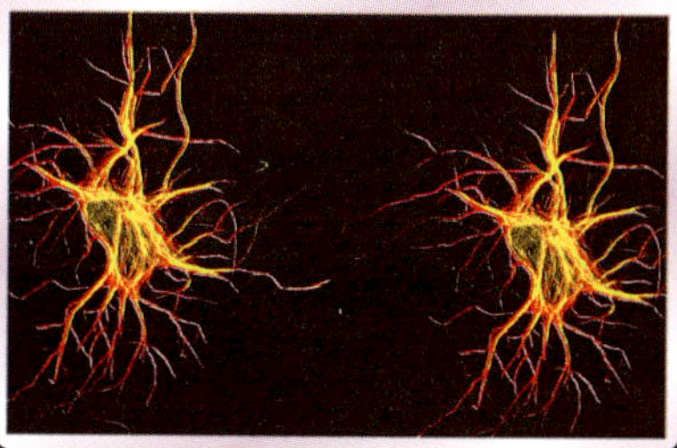

WHAT DO YOU KNOW ABOUT THE MUSCLES OF THE HEART?

The muscles which make up the heart are known as the cardiac muscles. The cardiac muscles are found only in the heart. These consist of a network of the branches of muscle fibres which have a striped

appearance. The cardiac muscles are involuntary in nature, which means that they are not under the control of the central nervous system. A contraction of the heart muscle originates an electrical impulse in a natural pacemaker called the sinoatrial node, which is located inside the heart. This sinoatrial node determines both the rhythm and rate of the heart. This node sends out regular electrical impulses to produce orderly contraction of the heart chambers. This, in turn, activates the sympathetic and parasympathetic nerves to increase or decrease the heart rate. A cardiac muscle is myogenic, meaning that it is self- excitable. It simulates contraction without a requisite electrical impulse coming from the central nervous system.

BITS OF FACT

There are about 639 muscles in the body. These muscles contain six thousand million muscle fibers and each fiber consists of 1,000 separate minute threads called fibrils.

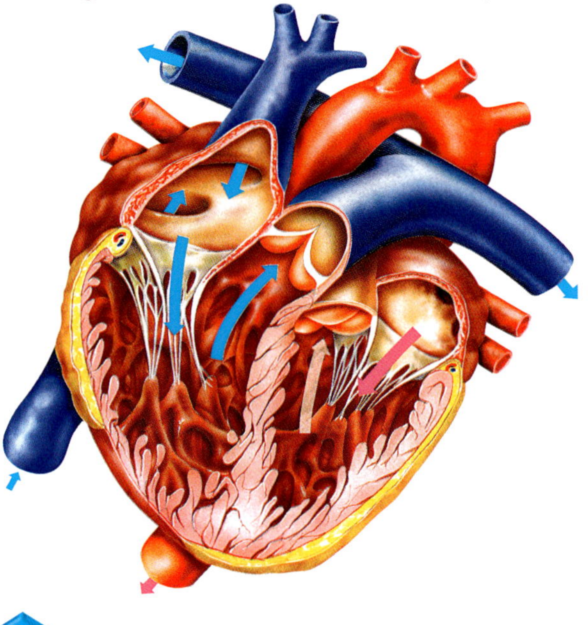

What do you know about funny bone?

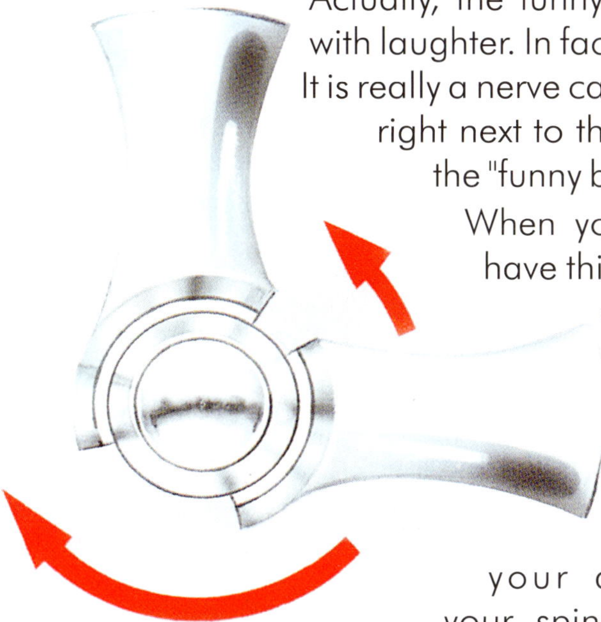

Actually, the funny bone has nothing to do with laughter. In fact, it isn't even a bone at all. It is really a nerve called the ulnar nerve. It runs right next to the "humerus". That's where the "funny bone" comes from.

When you bend your elbow, you have this ulnar nerver that is much easier to get to than most nerves are. So, when you hit your elbow, the nerve also gets whacked and begins to send messages that travel all the way up your arm to your spinal cord and along your spinal cord to your brain. It results in a tingling sensa-tion that shoots from your elbow, where the impact occurred, to the tip of your little finger which is where the nerve ends.

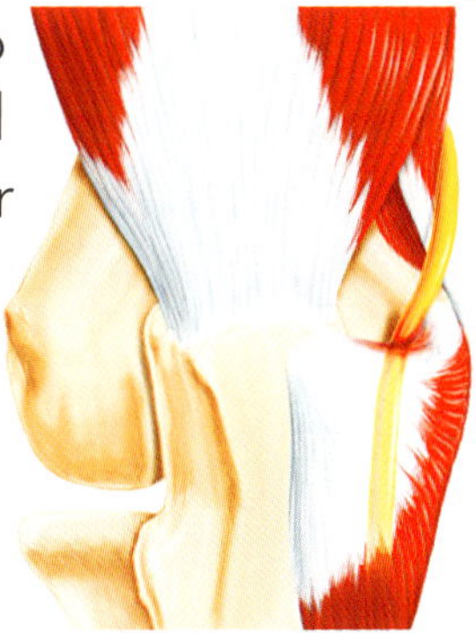

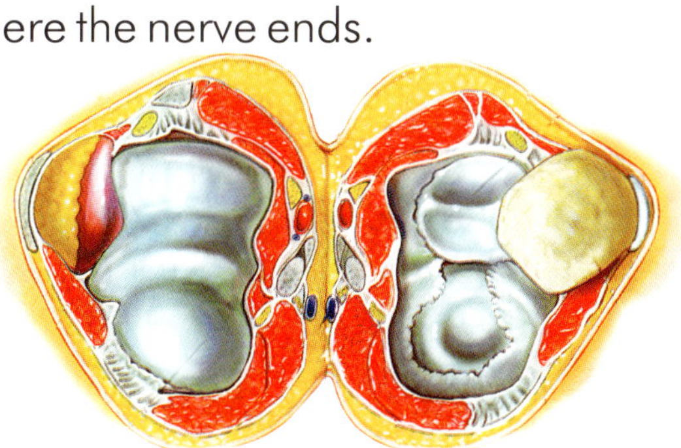

BITS OF FACT

Your bones consist of 50% water and 50% solid matter. The spine is special because it isn't made of one or even two bones – it's made of 26 bones in all. These bones are called vertebrae and each one is shaped like a ring.

WHAT DO YOU KNOW ABOUT THE APPENDIX?

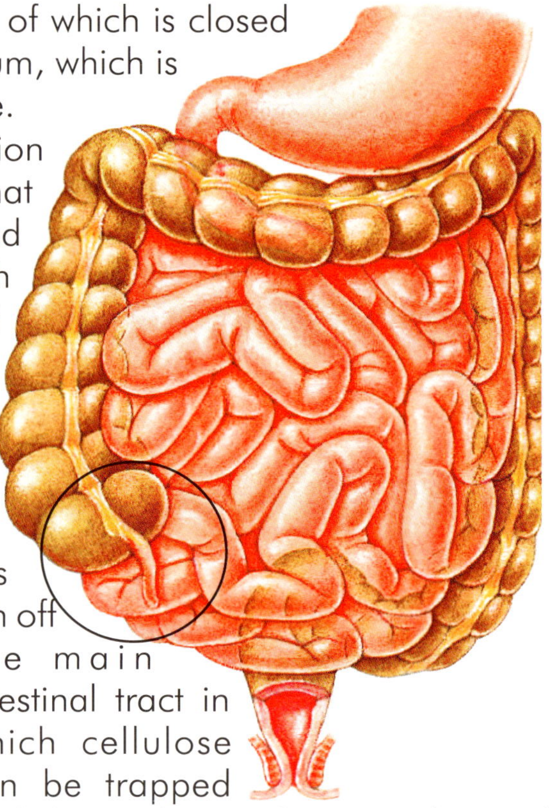

The appendix is a tube, one end of which is closed and the other opens into the cecum, which is the beginning of the large intestine. The appendix has no known function in a human. Evidence suggests that our evolutionary ancestors used their appendixes to digest tough food like tree barks, but we don't use ours in digestion now. It is believed that the appendix will gradually disappear in a human being as our diet does not include cellulose any more. In the other animals, the appendix is much larger and provides a pouch off the main intestinal tract in which cellulose can be trapped and be subjected to prolonged digestion. Indigestible food delivered from the small intestine to the large intestine flows into the appendix and is forced out by the contraction of the muscular walls of the appendix. A blockage in the opening, where the appendix attaches to the large intestine, can lead to the inflammation of the appendix, known as appendicitis. This can cause acute pain, fever, nausea, vomiting and loss of appetite. It can be cured easily by the removal of the appendix.

BITS OF FACT

Appendix is about the size of your longest finger. The first successful appendix operation was performed in Great Britain, over 250 years ago.

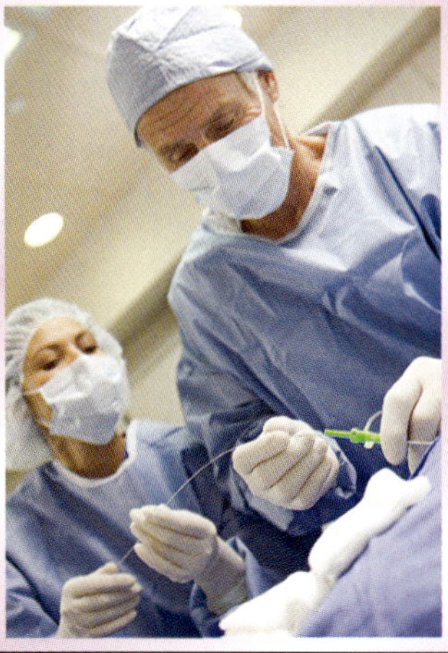

WHAT DO YOU KNOW ABOUT GIRAFFES?

Giraffe is the world's tallest animal with a height of about 5-6 m. But it is five times lighter than an elephant. Its long legs and neck help it to reach and eat the leaves, twigs and fruit at the top of trees, which other animals cannot eat. Apart from this, it has a 50 cm long, blue tongue which is so tough that it can wrap around the thorns of a thorny tree to get the twigs. The legs of the giraffe are about 2 m long, however, it consists of only seven bones–the same number of bones that a human has. The coat of the giraffe is patched in brown or cream. But each giraffe has its own unique pattern. The reticulated giraffes of East Africa have triangular patches, whereas the South African Cape giraffes have blotchy markings. When a giraffe walks, it moves its two legs on one side of its body and then the two on the other side. When it comes to running, it can gallop faster than the speediest racehorse with the help of its long legs.

BITS OF FACT

When a giraffe goes into a deep sleep - for about one minute at a time - it curls its neck back and rests its head on its rump. Giraffes sleep no more than 5 to 30 minutes in a 24-hour period.

WHAT DO YOU KNOW ABOUT THE TEETH OF CARNIVOROUS ANIMALS?

Carnivores are predators which catch and kill their prey before they can eat it. These carnivorous animals use their sharp claws to grip their prey. A big cat, such as a tiger, bites into the back of the neck of its prey. Its teeth move between the neck vertebrae and break the nerve cord connections to the brain. As a result, the prey dies instantly. The teeth of these carnivores are adapted to eat the flesh of their prey. At the front of the mouth, the teeth are sharp and pointed. There are four other teeth which are longer than the others. These are called the canine teeth. These are the teeth that the big cat uses to hold onto the throat of its prey to kill it. The teeth at the back of the mouth are also sharp and pointed but larger than those at the front. When the mouth is closed, these back teeth come together like the blades of a pair of scissors. These teeth are used to cut into the flesh of the prey and shear off the pieces of meat.

BITS OF FACT

Flesh eating animals that hunt in the cool climate at night and sleep during the day when it is hot do not need sweat glands to cool their bodies; they, therefore, do not perspire through their skins. On the contrary, they sweat through their tongues.

What do you know about the size of the heart of an animal?

The animal with the biggest heart is naturally the biggest animal ever - the blue whale. The heart of the blue whale is as big as a small car. Its main blood vessel is big enough to crawl through. But its heart beats very slowly, just five or six times per minute when the blue whale is at the surface and even slower when it dives. In comparison to this, a human heart beats seventy times per minute at rest. Above all, the heart of the hummingbird beats five hundred times per minute at rest and more than a thousand times per minute when it flies. Thus, the heart of the hummingbird is the largest in proportion when compared to any other animal's. An average mammal's heart comprises less than 1 per cent of its total body weight. The heart of a blue whale is only 0.5% of its body mass, whereas the heart of the hummingbird is 2% of its body mass. That is approximately 4% bigger than the whale's. This is because the humming-bird needs enough oxygen and food so that it may hover like a helicopter and remain in the sky for long hours.

BITS OF FACT

The animal with the highest normal blood pressure is the giraffe. However, the bird with the highest blood pressure is the flea, whose blood reaches a high pressure just before take-off for a big jump.

WHAT DO YOU KNOW ABOUT THE SURVIVAL OF THE ARCTIC FOX IN THE COLD?

The Arctic fox is a furry mammal that lives in the far north, in the tundra and coastal areas of North America, Iceland, Greenland, Scandinavia and Siberia. Towards the end of summer, the greyish brown coat of the Arctic fox begins to grow thicker. The colour of the fur turns grey and then white. This is how the Arctic fox gets well coated to help it survive the cold. Because of its thick coat, it is able to survive the freezing cold temperatures. Thick hair on the pads of its feet protects its feet from freezing and helps it to walk on the ice. The Arctic fox can walk on ice without slipping. It can curl up in the snow and cover its nose and face with its bushy tail to keep warm. The relatively small size of the Arctic fox's ears mimimizes heat loss. During summer, the fox hides food in its den or under rocks. In this way, it stores food for later use.

BITS OF FACT

The Arctic fox is the only mammal which is found in the far north (polar bears are partly aquatic). An arctic fox can catch small rodents and lemmings under the snow with its sharp curved claws and great hearing. It also has sharp teeth.

WHAT DO YOU KNOW ABOUT YAKS?

The yak is a long-haired humped domestic animal found in Tibet and throughout the Himalayan region of South Central Asia, as well as in Mongolia. Wild yaks are about two metres in height, whereas domestic yaks are about half that height. Both types have long shaggy hair to insulate them from the cold. Wild yaks can be either brown or black in colour. Domesticated ones can also be white in colour. Domestic yaks are kept for their milk, fibre and meat. Yak milk is often processed to cheese. Yaks are also used for transporting goods across mountain passes. Their dung is even burned to produce energy. Yak fibres are soft and smooth. They are of several colours, including grey, brown, black and white. The length of yak fibre is about 1.2 inches. It is combed or shed from the yak and then dehaired. This splendid downy fibre is spun into yarn and used for knitting. Many wild yaks are killed for food by the Tibetans.

BITS OF FACT

Nowadays, domesticated yaks are trained for sports like yak skiing or yak polo which have become a tourist attraction in Central Asian countries. Yaks secrete a special sticky substance in their sweat which helps keep their under-hair matted and acts as extra insulation. This secretion is used in traditional Nepalese medicine.

WHAT DO YOU KNOW ABOUT SNOW LEOPARDS?

A snow leopard is a medium-sized cat which weighs about 35 to 55 kilograms. Today, only a few hundred snow leopards are left which live in the Himalayas, where they are now a protected species. A snow leopard has a soft grey coat with ringed spots and rosettes of black or brown. Its tail is heavy with fur and the bottom of its paws is covered with fur for protection against snow and cold. These leopards come under the category of endangered species because their pelts command a very high price in the fur market. They are illegally hunted for their bones and body parts which are used in traditional Chinese medication. During the 1960s, their total population went down to 1,000. But it has recovered slightly since then. They are sparsely distributed across 12 countries in Central Asia: China, Bhutan, Nepal, India, Pakistan, Afghanistan, Tajikistan, Uzbekistan, Kyrgyzstan, Kazakhstan, Russia and Mongolia.

BITS OF FACT

Snow leopards have powerful legs and are tremendous leapers. They can jump up to 50 ft (15 m).

What do you know about prairie dogs?

A prairie dog is a mammal. It is about the size of a rabbit, which lives underground. It has a brown or grey-coloured coat with black-tipped hair and a black-tipped tail. The underside of the prairie dog is light tan in colour. It has short legs and sharp claws to help it dig its home. These mammals are found primarily in the prairies and they feed on grasses, roots, seeds and leafy plants. They dig tunnels and make small mounds around the entrance to the tunnels to prevent rain from entering them. Prairie dogs are organized into coteries. Each coterie usually consists of one male, three or four females and several young ones. Each female in a coterie produces one litter (2-10 pups) annually after a gestation period of 34 to 37 days. As many as two thousand prairie dogs may live in one prairie dog town. Farmers and ranchers have been known to poison prairie dogs because of the perceived threat to crops and livestock.

BITS OF FACT

Arctic ground squirrels make underground dens with lots of tunnels and rooms. They live in colonies. During spring and summer, they eat a lot to prepare themselves for a long sleep in winter. They are the only Arctic animals that hibernate.

WHAT DO YOU KNOW ABOUT DINGOES?

Dingoes are wild dogs found in Australia. They have features in common with both wolves and modern dogs and are regarded as

(more or less) the unchanged descendants of an early ancestor of modern dogs. They can be brown, black or white and usually live in packs. The main difference between a dingo and the other dogs is that dingoes do not bark. That doesn't mean that they remain silent. They howl and whine very loudly indeed. They have erect ears, larger canine teeth and domed heads. Unlike the domestic dog, a dingo breeds only once a year. The female dingo gives birth to about five pups, which are not independent until six to eight months of age. Dingoes eat rabbits, rodents, birds and lizards in addition to larger prey such as sheep and deer. Besides this, they even eat fruits and plants. Dingoes are considered a pest in Australia because of the large number of sheep and cattle they kill every year.

BITS OF FACT

Australian dingoes are larger than Asian dingoes. Wild Australian dingoes kill and eat prey ranging in sizes from small lizards, birds and rodents to sheep and kangaroos. They can also scavenge carrion.

What do you know about the art of snake charming?

There is a lot of misunderstanding about snake charming. Much of it is deliberately caused. A snake charmer likes us to believe that the snake is bewitched by the beautiful music it plays on his pipe. The snake sways and dances to the music while the charmer taps his foot on the ground in time with the rhythm. In fact, a snake is actually deaf; it cannot hear music. It doesn't respond to the sound of the pipe at all. It reacts to the vibrations it feels caused by charmer's tapping feet and appears to dance. The music has no part in it at all. A snake has no ear drum. Besides, it does not have the system of bones and ducts that convey the vibrations from the ear-drum to the sense cells of the inner ear.

BITS OF FACT

There are about 2,600 different kinds of snakes. Of these, about 400 are poisonous. The King Cobra is the largest of all venomous snakes, and actually eats other snakes.

What do you know about centipedes?

Centipedes are reddish-brown, flattened, elongated arthropods. The word 'Centipede' means 'hundred legged'. Actually, not many centipedes have as many as hundred legs. Some have as few as 15 pairs, others have as many as 173 pairs, but most centipedes have about 35 pairs. Both centipedes and millipedes form a small group of arthropods adapted for life on the land. They are generally about 1 or 2 inches long but species from North America can grow upto 7 inches long. A pair of legs is attached on most of its body segments. The first pair of legs located below the mouth is modified into poisonous jaws to kill insects. With all these legs, the centipede can run very quickly. Centipedes are usually found under the bark of fallen trees and under stones but sometimes they creep into our homes also. They feed on insects and other small animals but do not damage plants.

BITS OF FACT

The Amazonian giant centipede is the largest species of centipedes in the world. It reaches over 30 cm in length. It is known to eat bats, which it catches in midflight. It also eats rodents and spiders.

WHAT DO YOU KNOW ABOUT VENOMOUS FISH?

There are about 250 species of venomous fish. The most venomous fish is the stonefish. Stonefish are mottled greenish-brown in colour with their skins having many stone-like appendages which give them an almost perfect camouflage. The most striking feature of this species is its spine of 13 grooved hypodermic-like projections, each capable of piercing a sandshoe. If you accidentally step on one, the venomous spines on the back and sides of the stonefish will inject venom and cause severe pain, illness and perhaps death. Out of all the stonefish, the Reef Stonefish is the most venomous fish in the world. It is usually brown or grey and may have the patches of yellow, orange or red. It looks like an encrusted rock or lump of coral. It has thirteen stout spines in the dorsal fin which can inject a highly toxic venom. The venom causes intense pain and is believed to have killed many Pacific and Indian Ocean islanders.

BITS OF FACT

The box jellyfish is considered to be the world's most venomous marine creature. The box jellyfish has killed more people in Australia than stonefish, sharks and crocodiles combined.

What do you know about the menace of rabbits in Australia?

Rabbits have become a menace in Australia because they cause an enormous amount of damage to Australian farmlands. This is because they breed very quickly and eat almost any vegetable. In the 18th century, three pairs of rabbits were introduced into Australia. They multiplied so rapidly that, with the addition of others which were brought over, they spread over most of the continent and caused a tremendous amount of damage. The female rabbit or doe produces four to eight litters of five to eight young ones in a year. They are blind, helpless and nearly furless at birth. But in two weeks, they are able to run. In a month, they can fend for themselves. At the age of six months, they are able to breed. It is estimated that a pair of rabbits, given ideal conditions, could have 13,718,000 descendants in three years. Various attempts were made to control the rabbits but all in vain.

Finally, in the early 1950s a virus disease called myxamatosis was introduced. 80 per cent of the population of rabbits had died within three years.

BITS OF FACT

The smallest wild rabbit breed in North American is the Pygmy or Little Idaho rabbit, which weighs slightly less than one pound.

WHAT DO YOU KNOW ABOUT WOMBATS?

Wombats are stout, sturdy marsupials. They grow to about 1.3 m in length and can weigh up to 36 kg. They have large, blunt heads with small eyes and ears, and short, muscular necks. They have long, sharp claws and stubby, powerful legs which make them great diggers. Wombats live in burrows in usually well drained soils that are easy to dig in. The burrows, which are often built on the sides of gullies, can be up to 30 m long, and several m deep. A wombat can reproduce after it has reached two years of age. The young wombat weighs just 1 gm and is less than 3 cm long. It crawls from the birth canal to the mother's pouch. This pouch opens backwards, so when the mother is digging, she doesn't cover her baby with sand. In this way, she protects its young one from dirt and twigs. The young one stays in the pouch for about 10 months.

BITS OF FACT

The largest marsupial in the world is the Red Kangaroo. It is approximately 5 ft long and has a tail that is about 42 in long. It uses its tail for its balance mechanism. Red Kangaroos can't walk and are limited to hopping as a means of locomotion. They hop up to 30-40 miles per hour and leap over obstacles up to 10 ft high.

WHAT DO YOU KNOW ABOUT THE PLATYPUSES AND MAMMALS?

The platypus is a very special mammal. Usually, all mammals give birth to young ones but platypuses lay eggs. Mammals that lay eggs are called monotremes. Females lay up to 3 eggs. When they hatch, the

babies lick milk from a patch on their mother's stomach. The babies learn to look after themselves after about six months. They live along the banks of rivers and streams and spend a lot of time in the water. They are well adapted for living in water as they have thick coats of oily fur which keeps them warm if the water is really cold. Besides, they have strong webbed feet to pull them through the water when they are swimming. They use their tails for steering. The bill of a platypus is soft and rubbery and has 2 holes near the end which are the nostrils. The bill is very sensitive. The platypus uses it to feel for food on the riverbed. It likes to eat worms, shrimps and small crayfish.

BITS OF FACT

The only other monotreme besides the platypus is the echidna. Echidnas are covered with coarse hair and spines. The spines are made of the same substance as our own finger nails and the rhino's horn. An echidna's only form of defence is these spines. When threatened, it curls up in a ball to protect its soft underside or digs into the ground exposing only its spiny back.

WHAT DO YOU KNOW ABOUT THE ANIMALS THAT REGENERATE THEIR BODY PARTS?

Regeneration means the regrowing of a lost or damaged limb. Among invertebrates, the capacity to regenerate parts like legs or entire sections of the body is fairly common. The planarians (flat worms) can be cut into 50 pieces and you will end up with 50 smaller worms. If an arm of a starfish is cut off, you will have two starfishes after regeneration. Crickets can regenerate their legs. These are just a few examples of invertebrates capable of regenerating their complex structures. There is only one group of vertebrates that has the capacity to regenerate their highly complex structures such as limbs, jaws, tails, spinal cords or eyes throughout their lives: the urodele amphibians. Urodeles are salamanders and have the outstanding ability to regenerate perfectly their complex tissues over and over again. Each time, the regenerated tissue is identical to the original in appearance and function. A lizard often sheds its tail to escape its predator. The tail regrows, but it is not a perfect replacement of the original. If a lizard loses a leg, it will never regrow. Frogs, meanwhile, can regenerate their tails as tadpoles, but they lose all their regenerative capacity after metamorphosis.

BITS OF FACT

If a crayfish loses a claw, the missing claw will grow back during the next molt (when an animal molts, it sheds its hard outer skin or shell and replaces it with a new one).

WHAT DO YOU KNOW ABOUT THE ANIMAL THAT HAS THE LARGEST EYES?

The eyes of the giant squid (Architeuthis dux) can be up to 25 centimetres (ten inches) across, about the size of a volleyball. Those large, sensitive eyes are useful in the dark waters where the giant squid lives, about 200-700 metres (660-2,300 feet) below the surface of the ocean. Giant squids are among the world's most mysterious large animals. No live specimen has been captured so far. Like all squids, a giant squid has a mantle (torso), eight arms and two longer tentacles. The arms and tentacles account for much of the squid's great length. It is a deep ocean animal that can grow to a tremendous size. Recent estimates put the maximum size at 13 metres for a female squid and 10 metres for a male squid. A giant squid has small fins at the rear of the mantle. It uses these fins for locomotion. It has a complex, well-developed brain. It is a ferocious predator. It is pursued and eaten by large cetaceans such as sperm whales.

BITS OF FACT

The hawk has the sharpest eyes. Each of its eyes is endowed with fovea where vision is sharpest.

WHAT DO YOU KNOW ABOUT THE ANIMAL THAT CHEWS ITS FOOD WITH ITS LEGS?

The horseshoe crab does not have jaws and teeth. It usually chews its food with its legs. However, it does not need its legs to grind food because, like birds, it has a crop that breaks down food before it passes through the gut. While the horseshoe crab does not have a conventional jaw, its four pairs of walking legs have a special equipment attached to them. The crab uses it to manipulate and shred food before passing it to its mouth. The last pair of walking legs can be used to break shells and to crush tough food. Because the crab often swallows sand and shell fragments, its gizzard (stomach) is quite powerful and can grind up almost anything it consumes.

The horseshoe crab has millions of sensors scattered over its body with the help of which it can smell worms in the water. Then, it follows them, grabs them with its front leg-like pincers and stuffs them live into a hole in its oesophagus. Bristly spines on its walking legs that surround the mouth grind the food.

BITS OF FACT

Horseshoe crabs are among the world's oldest and most fascinating creatures. They are estimated to be at least 300 million years old. They are really not crabs at all; they are distant relatives of the spider that belongs to an ancient arthropod group. This arthropod group existed for over 400 million years.

What do you know about the mammals that have the shortest and longest gestation periods?

Gestation is the period of time between fertilization and the birth of a mammal. The shortest known gestation period is 12 to 13 days. This record is shared by three marsupials (mammals in which the young ones are born prematurely and finish developing in a pouch located near the mother's abdomen). They are the American or Virginian opossum (Didelphis marsupialis), the rare water opossum or yapok (Chironectes minimus) of northern South America and the eastern native cat (Dasyurus viverrinus) of Australia. All three of these marsupials give birth to their young ones. The young ones, then, find their way to a small pouch where they mature, like a baby kangaroo. This pouch stage lasts up to two months after which they stay close to their mothers for another month or so.

The longest gestation period for a mammal is that of the African elephant *(Loxodonta africana)* with a period from 660 days to 760 days. These elephants carry their babies in their wombs for about 660 days or 22 months.

BITS OF FACT

Camels and giraffes carry their babies for about 400 days. Other animals that have gestation periods closest to that of humans are: dolphins - 276 days, chimpanzees - 237 days and cattle - 280 days.

WHAT DO YOU KNOW ABOUT THE ABSORPTION OF WATER BY PLANTS?

It is true that plants need a lot of water to stay healthy. Plants are mostly made of water. A pumpkin, for example, is 94% water. If we do not water plants, they will wilt and eventually die. Most of the water we give to a plant does not stay in its body. The water passes through the plant and evaporates into the air. Plants absorb most of their water through their roots. If you observe the ends of the roots carefully you will see that they look furry. This 'fur' is made of the root hair. This is where most of the water is absorbed. From the roots, the water travels up the stem in very thin tubes or vessels. Then, it moves towards the leaves. The water travelling through a plant and the substances dissolved in it is called sap. Eventually, the water arrives in the leaf where it escapes into the air as water vapour. The evaporation of water from the leaves of plants is called transpiration. The water vapour passes through microscopic pores in the leaf surface called stomata.

BITS OF FACT

The roots of a plant can be very extensive. Roots up to 50 kilometres of area can be found in one square metre of soil. A single wheat plant has a total of 70 km of roots and a single rye plant has a total of 80 km of roots.

WHAT DO YOU KNOW ABOUT CARNIVOROUS PLANTS?

There are some plants which capture and eat insects. Still, they are green in colour. This is because these plants grow in the soil which is very poor in mineral content, especially nitrogen and phosphorus. These plants, called carnivorous plants, make organic matter for their bodies by photo-synthesis and they eat insects to obtain certain minerals. The sundew is a carnivorous plant which is found in Europe. It has leaves which are brightly coloured to attract the insects. These leaves are also covered with sticky hair which traps the insects which land on them. The pitcher plant is another carnivorous plant. Its leaves are shaped like tubes, which collect rain water. There is a sweet substance around the rim of each tube which attracts insects. Once the insect has entered the tube, it is prevented from escaping by small, slippery hair which points downwards. Eventually, the insect exhausts itself by its effort to escape and slides into the water. The pitcher plant releases juices which digest the insect.

BITS OF FACT

The leaves of Venus Fly-trap open wide. There are short, stiff hair called trigger or sensitive hair on them. When anything touches the hair again and again, the two lobes of the leaves snap shut and trap whatever is inside. The trap shuts in less than a second. If the object isn't food, e.g., a stone or a nut, the trap reopens in about twelve hours and spits it out.

WHAT DO YOU KNOW ABOUT THE SURVIVAL OF PLANTS DURING WINTERS?

It is difficult for plants to survive in winters. The days are shorter and there is less sunlight. The cold temperature slows down their growth. Often, the temperature drops below zero degree, freezes the water and makes it inaccessible to plants. Such conditions are sure to kill all plants if they do not have techniques for survival. Some plants enter a resting stage. The plants which show new growth above ground year after year are called perennial plants. The part of each of these plants above ground dies over the winter months, while underground storage organs assure the survival of that plant for the following spring. A bulb is an example of an underground storage organ. Annual plants are those which live for only one year. In the cold winter months, only their seeds survive and the plants grow when spring comes. Sunflowers are considered annuals because they grow for one year and die. Each flower leaves behind many seeds which can grow into new plants.

BITS OF FACT

The hurricane plant has holes in its leaves, which keep it from being destroyed by wind.

WHAT DO YOU KNOW ABOUT THE GERMINATION OF SEEDS?

In general, most seeds germinate at temperatures between 10°C and 35°C. Some seeds, however, need a period of cold conditions before they germinate. For example, cherry seeds germinate better if they are kept humid at 5°C, for 16 weeks. If these seeds are kept at 25°C, they do not germinate. Water is also important for the germination of seeds. A light fall of rain may be enough to start the germination of some seeds. For desert plants, the seeds often need to be soaked for several hours before they germinate. Most seeds germinate quite easily in the dark. Some seeds, however, need to be exposed to the light for a certain time before they germinate. For example, the seeds of the birch tree need 8 successive days and about 10 hours of sunlight before they germinate. The seed coat or testa which protects the seed from damage or disease is often hard and waterproof. Some seeds do not germinate until the seed coat has been removed. Once the seed coat is removed, water enters and the embryo starts respiring. The seed coat may get removed when the soil particles rub against the seed coat and wear it away.

BITS OF FACT

The viability of seeds (their capacity to sprout) ranges from a few weeks (orchid) to over 400 years (Indian lotus) and up to 10,000 years (Arctic lupine).

What do you know about the transport of water from roots to the top in the giant redwood tree?

A redwood reaches a height of about 100 metres which is as tall as a 30-storey building. It has a system of inter-connected wood cells for carrying water. The hollow, short, thin cells are stacked intricately to form an incredibly tall column. These cells are dead wood that function as pipes with pitted openings along the sides of the pipe for water to pass between adjacent cells. The small cells rarely exceed a quarter of an inch in length. These form a continuous column of water within this pipe in order to move water through the pipe. Two forces move the water: a push and a pull. Roots do most of the pushing and leaves do most of the pulling. Water which evaporates from the leaves starts the suction process. Water molecules evaporate from a leaf and pull on the molecules around it as they depart. This creates a small suction in the water column and pulls water from adjacent water-conducting leaf cells. These molecules, in turn, attract those around them. The chain continues to the ground and moves water from the roots to the tree top.

BITS OF FACT

The largest tree of the redwood family is 272 feet high and has a circumference at the base of its trunk of 101 feet. Its weight has been estimated to be over 6,000 tons.

What do you know about the most poisonous plant?

The castor bean plant is the most deadly of all plants. If you eat a single castor bean or say two, you may die. If you live beyond three to five days, you will probably survive. Castor beans (not true beans, but rather seeds) contain a poison, called ricin. If eaten it prevents the cells of the body from making proteins. Cells die without the proteins. The resulting damage to the body can be great enough to kill a person eventually. The stalked leaves of the castor bean plant consist of eight radiating, pointed leaflets with slightly serrated edges and prominent central veins. Many varieties are green, but some are reddish-brown. The flowers are green and inconspicuous, but pink or red in the pigmented varieties. Castor beans are pressed to extract castor oil which is used for medicinal purposes.

BITS OF FACT

The seeds of an apple contain a toxin, cyanogenic acids. It they are taken in a large amount, they could prove fatal to humans and animals. Luckily, the seeds from just one or two apples aren't enough; you would need a lot of apples to gather enough seeds to make them deadly.

What do you know about peanuts?

Peanuts grow well in any sandy place where it's warm for 120 to 140 days, moderately rainy (25 to 50 inches yearly) and no frost. The plant originated in South America, perhaps Brazil or Bolivia. Now, it is grown worldwide. Farmers plant peanuts by seed. The seed sprouts, grows about 18 inches and bears light green leaves. Yellow flowers appear and bloom for about a month. The plant pollinates itself usually, but occasionally, bees transfer the pollen to another plant. After fertilization, the flowers fade and the young fruit forms a pointed stalk called a peg. The peg points and grows downwards. The fruits (*i.e.* peanuts) develop woody outer shells (the peanut shells). Then, the pointed fruits bury themselves in the ground. They continue to mature underground but ripen at different times–anywhere from 90 to over 150 days. Afterwards, they are harvested.

BITS OF FACT

Records indicate the good old peanut has been around for 3500 years or so. The first major use of peanuts was as food for pigs. The first notable use of peanuts as food for humans came during the Civil War, when both the Northern and Southern troops used peanuts as a source of food during hard times.

What do you know about the oldest living cloned plant on the Earth?

King's holly (Lomatia tasmanica) is the oldest living cloned plant on the Earth. This plant is 43,600 years old. In 1937, Deny King discovered the plant while mining tin by hand in the remote southwest of Tasmania. The plant was named in the King's honour. This plant has shiny green leaves and bears pink flowers, but yields neither fruit nor seeds. All the plants of this species are technically separate. Each of these plants has its own root system. It reproduces itself by dropping branch pieces that take roots. It can only reproduce itself by cloning genetically identical bushes. Investigators have found the fossil of the leaf fragments identical to the living bush 5.3 miles (8.5 km) away. The cell structure and shape of the fossil are the same as those of the living plant. It means this ancient plant was triploid (having three times the haploid number of chromosomes) also. The life-span of King's holly is approximately 300 years, but the plant has been cloning itself for at least 43,600 years.

BITS OF FACT

The oldest living flowering shrubs, called creosote bushes, on the earth are 12,000 years old. They are located in the Mojave Desert.

WHAT DO YOU KNOW ABOUT THE SURVIVAL OF A FOREST AFTER A FIRE?

After a fire has occurred, the soil becomes less acidic and the amount of nutrients available to plants always increase. That is why plants re-grow quickly after a fire. Fires usually occur in the evergreen forests of pines, spruces and firs which grow in hot, dry countries. Fires don't burn everything uniformly. 5 % of these forests escape the fire probably because of the wet land. These patches provide seeds for the re-growth. Red and white pine trees branch high above the ground, away from a seething surface fire. Moreover, their thick bark can withstand low-level fires and, hence, they survive such fires. Seeds in Jack-pine cones can withstand temperatures of 900° Celsius (1,700 ° Fahrenheit) for short times. Warmth from the fire encourages the cones to open and release seeds. Within five to ten years, the forest is re-seeded. White birch and trembling aspen re-sprout from their roots, even if badly burned.

BITS OF FACT

Rehabilitating tens of millions of hectares of degraded land and reforesting the Earth is necessary to restore and maintain the productivity of soil and water resources.

What do you know about reproduction in plants by themselves?

Many plants can propogate themselves by vegetative reproduction. In this process, part of a plant separates off, takes root and grows into a new plant. It is a process by which a new plant arises without the

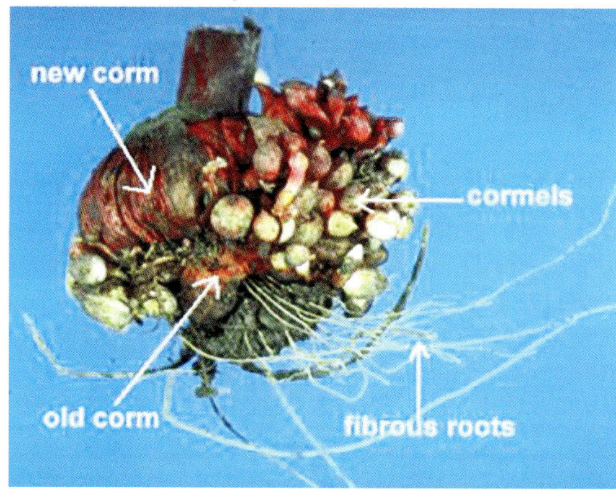

production of seeds. It is found mostly in herbaceous plants and involves structural modifications of the stem, roots and in some cases the leaf also. Some plants produce bulbils or small bulbs that develop on the stem or in the place of flowers. These bulbils drop off and grow into new plants. Similarly, some plants use underground storage organs. Such organs include rhizomes (horizontal, underground stems) like ginger, the branches of which produce new plants. Corms which separate from the parent grow into new plants. Other propogative structures are runners and stolons which are creeping horizontal stems that take roots and produce new plants.

BITS OF FACT

Grafting is the process of attaching a shoot (or less frequently a bud) from an individual plant you want to clone to the root stock of another tree. It is the only available method of cloning the older trees of many species.

WHAT DO YOU KNOW ABOUT UNDERWATER PLANTS?

Plants which grow submerged in water are called wetland plants or

hydrophytes. Some plants may grow partially in water like the water hyacinth and some plants may grow completely in water like the pond weed. These plants have special adaptations to survive in this habitat. They have numerous air spaces inside their stems, leaves and roots which help exchange gases in addition to providing buoyancy. Submerged plants generally have no cuticles or waterproof coverings. This enables them to absorb minerals and gases directly from the water. The primary function of cuticles is to prevent water loss. Thus, most hydrophytes have no need for cuticles. The gas-exchange pores or stomata are not present in the plants that are completely submerged in water. Whereas, in partially submerged plants with floating leaves like the water lilies, stomata are found on the upper leaf surfaces.

BITS OF FACT

Water hyacinths are floating plants with round to oval, shiny green leaves which are up to ten inches in diameter. Leaves are held upright, so they act like sails. The leaf stalk is thick and spongy and helps to keep the plant buoyant. A mass of fine roots hangs in the water underneath the plant.

WHAT DO YOU KNOW ABOUT EPIPHYTIC AND PARASITIC PLANTS?

Both epiphytic and parasitic plants grow on other living plants, but there are some differences. Epiphytic plants live above the ground level on the stems and branches of other plants. They get their supply of water from trapped rainwater and moisture in the air. Besides, they get minerals from the organic matter that collects on the surface of the plant on which they grow. Like other green plants, they manufacture their own food by photosynthesis. Examples of epiphytes are tropical orchids, bromelaids and some mosses that live in temperate regions. Parasitic plants get all their nutrient requirements from the plants on which they grow. They produce root-like organs which penetrate the stems or roots of the host plants. Then, they grow inwards and merge with the vascular tissues of the host plants from which they get their supply of water and minerals. Fully parasitic plants lack chlorophyll, but partially parasitic plants like the mistletoe have green leaves and, hence, produce their own food by photosynthesis.

BITS OF FACT

Epiphytic ferns are one of the most common features in rainforests. They grow on the trunks and limbs of trees but (unlike parasitic plants such as mistletoe) they do not steal nutrients from their host tree. Instead, they survive on rainwater and the nutrients they get from the trapped fallen leaves.

What do you know about cinchona trees?

The cinchona tree is a tropical tree which grows from 5 to 15 metres in height. It is an evergreen tree with broad and flat leaves with a shiny green surface and large veins. The flowers are white and elongated, covered thickly with silky hair. The cinchona tree is native to the rainforests of the eastern slope of the Amazonian Andes of South America, where it is called the "fever tree". It is called so because it is the primary source of the anit-malarial drug, *i.e.* quinine. Quinine is a chemical that cures malaria. It is found in the bark of the cinchona tree. People in Peru still use the cinchona as the best remedy for fevers, digestive problems and infections. As a bitter tonic, cinchona stimulates saliva, digestive secretions and appetite. Moreover, it improves the weak digestive function. It is also used in making gargles for sore, and infected throats. In India, cinchona is used to treat sciatica (pain, numbness or weakness that travels from the low back through the buttocks and down the large sciatic nerve in the back of the leg) and dysentery.

BITS OF FACT

An average-sized tree produces enough oxygen in one year to keep a family of four breathing.

WHAT DO YOU KNOW ABOUT BAMBOO PLANTS?

Bamboo, a plant of the family Gramineae, is the longest grass in the world. Some bamboo plants are as short as 30 cm, while giant timber bamboo can grow to a height of over 40 metres or 100 feet. A bamboo plant consists of a hollow culm or stem with nodes or joints between the segments of the stem, and oval leaves. It is also perhaps the fastest growing plant with some varieties growing at the rate of 5 cm per hour or 1.5 metres a day. Within a few months, new shoots of the Moso species grow up to a height of 12 to 15 metres. New shoots of some of the larger species can grow over 1 metre per day. Once a bamboo shoot has reached full height and produces leaves, it never gets any taller. The bamboo plant has a wide variety of uses, ranging from being purely decorative to being an important source of fuel. It is utilised as wood in construction work, furniture, utensils, fibre and paper. Bamboo charcoal makes a good fuel because it is three times as porous as wood, and releases more energy. Bamboo shoots are also delicious to eat, whereas the leaves provide fodder for animals like the panda.

BITS OF FACT

In 1974, it was noted that an Albizzia falcata tree in Sabah, Malaysia, had grown 35 feet and 3 inches in 13 months, approximately 1.1 inches per day.

WHAT DO YOU KNOW ABOUT THE PLANTS THAT EXISTED DURING THE DAYS OF DINOSAURS AND STILL LIVE TODAY IN THEIR ORIGINAL FORM?

Dinosaurs roamed the land from 225 to 65 million years ago. During that time, different plants evolved and some, like seed ferns, also died out. Others like mosses, horse tails, ferns, conifers, cycads, magnolias lasted for long and remained unchanged. Mosses edged from the sea onto lava-strewn land, almost 500 million years ago, but were severely handicapped. They had no roots and still don't. Then around 400 million years ago, there came a group of three plants–Club mosses, horse tails and ferns–with roots. The herds of long-necked Sauropod dinosaurs fed on the ferns. The descendants of these plants thrive today without much change. The club mosses and horse tails grew tall (100 feet, 30m). Seeds evolved next, about 225 million years ago. Conifers and cycad trees were among the first plants to produce seeds. Camarasaurs and Brachiosaurs hacked these early trees off with their blade-like teeth. These dinosaurs had steel-lined stomachs. Today, no mammal eats conifers because of their foul-tasting, toxic sap. Dinosaurs were alive around 100 million years ago when the first flowering plants appeared. Magnolias flourish today much as they did when dinosaurs roamed.

BITS OF FACT

Pine, spruce or other evergreen wood should never be used for barbecuing. These woods, while letting out smoke, can add harmful tar and resins to the food. Only hardwoods should be used for grilling meat, such as oak, pecan, hickory, maple, cherry, alder, apple or mesquite, depending on the type of meat being cooked.

WHAT DO YOU KNOW ABOUT THE PLANTS THAT APPEAR TO FLOAT ON WATER?

Some water plants are rooted in the mud and have their leaves above the surface. Such plants appear to float on water. The water lily, also known as pond lily, is a large aquatic plant which appears to float on water. The long, strong leaves and flower stalks of the water lily rise from the muddy bottom below. The leaves are kidney-shaped and are usually seen floating on the surface of water, but may also be submerged. Giant water lilies have huge leaves with the edges upturned like shallow pans to keep them afloat. The leaves of the Royal or Amazon lily can be 2 metres across. The flowers may be 30 cm across. Another grass-like water plant that grows on River Nile is the papyrus. Ancient Egyptians flattened their stems to write on. The word 'paper' comes from papyrus. Some species of buttercup float slightly submerged in water; only the flowers extend above the water. Their leaves and roots are long and thin and almost hair-like. The long roots and thin leaves also provide a greater surface area for the uptake of mineral solutes and oxygen.

BITS OF FACT

Water hyacinths are American water flowers which grow very quickly and can even clog up slow streams. Mexico's largest lake, Lake Chapala, gets sometime choked with water hyacinths.

WHAT DO YOU KNOW ABOUT THE SURVIVAL OF PLANTS IN DESERTS?

Plants which grow in dry regions are known as xerophilous. The roots of these plants spread out horizontally close to the surface of the soil. In this way, the roots can soak up whatever rain falls before the the heat of the Sun evaporates all the moisture. Some roots go down deep into the soil to search for damper places. The stalks of desert plants have no leaves and are covered with waxy materials which prevent moisture from evaporating from the plants. These plants are even covered with sharp thorns or spines to stop animals from eating them. Many plants produce beautiful flowers and fruits after rains. The stems of most cacti are massive and can store large amounts of water that sustain the plants during prolonged drought. Cacti have thick waxy cuticles on their stems, which act as waterproofing skins. Also, the pores called stomata in the cactus skin that are necessary for the uptake of carbon dioxide tend to open only at night. As a result, very little water is lost.

BITS OF FACT

The creosote bush is a large shrub and has small, round leaves which look and feel oily or sticky. This coating called 'lac' helps to keep water from being lost to the dry air.

What do you know about the various uses of ebony?

Ebony is the hard black wood of various tropical trees marked for their hard and beautiful wood. There are more than 300 species of ebony, ranging in sizes from shrubs to trees, taller than 100 ft (30 m). The best commercial ebony comes from India, Madagascar, Nigeria, Zaire and the Celebes Islands. Only the black or brown heartwood is used commercially. The leaves of the plant are broad and vary in length according to the size of the plant. The flowers are white or greenish-white, which are eaten by animals and humans because of their sweetness when ripe. The leaves and other parts of the tree are used in traditional medicine to treat intestinal parasites, wounds, dysentery and fever. The wood of the ebony is very dense. It is used for many purposes, including tool and knife handles, furniture, inlay work, wall panelling, golf club heads and musical instruments. For many years, ebony had been used for making the black keys on the piano.

BITS OF FACT

The African ebony is prized for its intensely black core. With a wood-density of 64 lb/cu. ft (1,030 kg/cu. m), it has a specific gravity of 1.03 . It is found in Cameroon, Ghana, Nigeria and Zaire.